I0087058

THREE YEARS DREAMING:

A MEMOIR

By Matthew Howard

puma concolor aeternus press
2015

Three Years Dreaming: A Memoir.

Paperback Edition ISBN-10: 0692368094
Paperback Edition ISBN-13: 9780692368091
Kindle Ebook Edition ASIN: B00SCFLF9K

Contents

Introduction

That night, you go to sleep.

You enter the house of endless rooms. You get lost at first, but finally stumble into the hallway you seek. There, in the wall, you see the door to the basement.

The door shuts behind you as you walk down the stone stairs. A fire burns brightly in a fireplace, heating an iron cauldron. You have no trouble finding your way around the basement this time.

Here it is. Right here on this table: the book.

As you pick it up, you remember how many times you looked for it, over and over, in other dreams. Here it was, all along. Its pages contain three years of your dream memories. All those secrets you learned. All those adventures you forgot about the next day.

You open it to the first page.

Year One

Later, the two of you go for a drive. She's got the wheel. You had an appointment somewhere, but she wanted to go for a drive. You know you'll miss the appointment. She smiles wickedly and tells you how much fun it is going to be.

It is.

In the late afternoon or early evening, the two of you sit together on your couch in a classic urban loft with huge windows that let in natural light. There's a large bathtub with an open room all to itself, like a giant spa made of stone. You are drawn to her, and she is drawn to you, and it feels heavenly.

5/22

At the supermarket counter, you find a bin with a medium sized black seal sitting in it. The skin is the texture of Mystique's skin from the *X-Men* movie, but rubbery. It must be cold, because you have on a bulky outfit and gloves.

You squeeze the seal. It seems filled with a viscous red gel instead of bones and organs. It is alive. You choose it to be *your* seal. That means the butcher will kill it for you and give you the meat.

You like the seal and feel it would be a shame to kill it. It's a nice seal. But the decision has already been made. It will be carried out regardless. You are hungry, after all.

If the seal were not so fascinatingly cool and beautiful, or if it were a dog or pig or chicken, you would say,

"Whatever, kill the fucking thing. I'm hungry." But instead you just feel bad. You hand him over to the butcher but don't watch.

6/10

You and your GF got to a large building where a convention on tantra and sexuality is being held. Although you are allowed into the building, there's some reason the two of you cannot join the convention itself. Could it be a problem with your tickets?

The two of you hang out on the fringes. Soon, there's an opportunity to go in, a brief chance to sneak in. You follow the hallways to a room where a small group sits on the floor around a low rectangular table, almost Japanese-style seating. Beyond the table is a small shelving unit or box.

You crawl towards it this box on the floor on your belly like a snake. You are looking for something. Your GF and the group watch you do this.

Then, you wander around the interior of the building. It doesn't seem like much of a convention. Just some weird semi-dark hallways and rooms, and not a lot of people. No one is having sex.

Later, you are at the airport. It's brightly lit from many windows. A group of people sit in chairs in the waiting area. You play with a little blonde girl. The two of you laugh at some video game played on a little console you share. You give her a hug, and she kisses you. You feel embarrassed.

Date Unknown

Your employer shows you how to build a giant open-air barn/greenhouse. You use a vacuum to suck dusty old insulation off the underside of the roof's overhang. He's up on the roof talking about how big a project this is. There's a small shed or house in the corner. Your employer says he think it's entirely possible for you to put a roof that's just as good on the huge house.

Date Unknown

You ride your bicycle to meet your GF. She's wearing an outfit like she would have worn in high school. Lots of decorations, hair spiked to the side, striped jacket.

The two of you get inside a fence at a power plant. You start messing with the core of an electrical power generator. You end up spilling water on it and smashing it with the bike. Electric sparks fly everywhere. The two of you escape through a broken hole in the fence.

She takes your arm, and you stroll up to a party. You sport black fingernail polish and black dyed hair. Together you sip your martinis and cocktails.

Just ahead are a future GF and the Russian kid walking arm-in-arm like you are. The four of you chat amicably and head off to refill your drinks at the bar.

The bar is more like a cooking island from a kitchen. The dark-skinned man appears, and you spill your drinks. As the liquid seeps into the ground, the outdoor party transforms into an underground basement party. Sections of the floor are coming up. You see a layer of large insect eggs/larvae arranged in neat rows and columns. These are giant ant eggs!

Just then, a herd of giant ants comes up to grab the eggs and relocate them to safety. In the next room, you find even bigger eggs. Larger than footballs. And a huge black ant the size of a Great Dane stands there. Scary as he seems, he's just concerned with protecting the ant eggs. You don't mess with him, and he doesn't mess with you. But his jaws click and clack in a menacing way as if to say he can chop you in half with his face. Ants and eggs scurry everywhere.

Date Unknown

In your aquarium, you have two fish. A third fish—a mudskipper—and a lizard are there, too. The fish and the mudskipper are dying. You dump them into the trash, using a net to scoop them out of the tank. You save the lizard and the fish.

But, you have a terrible feeling that maybe the other animals weren't dead. Maybe you threw them out when they were still alive. You imagine them gasping and choking.

Go to the trash can. Look for them. But you already took them all the way out to the dumpster!

What a way to ruin a night that started off reading comic books with your GF. You had just got a bunch of new posters and were taping the posters all over your office. *Dreadstar*. *Robocop*. Stuff like that. Cool stuff.

Date Unknown

Dad takes you to the police station with him. He's interviewing someone and collecting evidence. You walk around for a bit.

Look! There's a guy being chased! He jumps in a small propeller plane and rams the pursuers' car, sending both of them off the road and into a small river by the roadside. These chase scenes are better than *Death Race 2000*!

You walk down to the river and talk to the guy like you know him. The plane is over a storm drain. The two of you talk about the demise of the guy in the car. You know his name. He's dead now, under the water.

You reach into the storm drain and pull out a small plastic T. Rex figurine. You tell the pilot, "Now whenever we see the dinosaur, we can think of him. We have something to remember him by."

8/28

You and your sister are packing up your stuff to move out of your childhood house. Everything goes in a huge yellow moving truck in the gravel driveway.

Your verbal disagreement ends with her screaming an amazing loud scream. Mom and Dad show up. We don't have a lot of time. We need to be in our new place and have the truck back by a certain time. And if we're late, it will cost more money.

Mom and Dad don't take you to your new apartments, though. Instead, you end up at a little old house with some weird old people, hanging out until dark. You have to remind them that we have a time limit and need to get going!

9/5

In the neighborhood you lived in as an adolescent, you drive around with this guy who tells you that since he's going to be gone for a while, you can borrow his personal assistant, Bill.

You, Bill, and your GF go out for a night on the town. You hit a bar in Phoenix and a bar in your old neighborhood. Your GF's on crutches. You two talk a lot and go outside to talk by the parking lot. Then she wants you to go.

At the car, she gets in the back seat with her crutches. She lies on her back in the back seat. She seems drunk, but you don't think she really is. "What's wrong?" you say. "Did the two guys by the door say something to you when you walked by?" She says, "Yes, but that's not it."

Bill helps you out with her. He isn't always right beside you, but he appears at certain moments when you need him. Pretty neat personal assistant! GF is in the back seat now, stroking her vulva through her panties. It's really turning you on, but it's time to go.

Then it's bright daylight and GF is in the driver's seat. You ride in back. An amazing desert landscape stretches out in all directions. You try to take in all the views, but GF keeps turning around and talking to you instead of watching where she's going.

You drive by incredible mountains, craters, volcanoes spewing black clouds of ash and smoke into the air. Rock formations sculpt abstract figures into pinnacles. Smoke, thick, slow, rolling, translucent. GF says, "There's a formation here called the crater of Venus."

As you continue past this display of rugged natural beauty, the landscape transforms into your adolescent home. GF is still turning around to talk to you. You yell at her, "Just Drive! Yes, it's a great view. I'm trying to enjoy it, but you are making me nervous not watching what you're doing! Just turn around and pay attention to driving!"

She pouts for a minute. Bill appears in the front passenger seat. The car pulls up beside your adolescent home. The three of you discuss that Bill has no problems. He has this personal assistant gig for some rich dude. You tell him he'd have to have pancreatic cancer to have any problems. Just trying to think of something really bad, but then you feel like a freak for saying it. For a minute, you forget Bill's name. Then, "Bill," you say, "This is the first time in this dream that your name has been spoken."

You get out of the car. On the floor behind the driver's seat lie packets of coupons. You pick one out for GF. Bill's got a bunch of Pizza Hut coupons for her, you say. It's a pretty big packet of coupons, like the size of a newspaper.

Bill. What a guy. He's got a way with the ladies, and no worries to speak of other than his personal assistant gig, which seems to have a lot of time off. And he's handy. He's there to help you out. He seems calm and cool and reasonable. He only appears when things with the GF get out of hand. Helping her in the backseat when she's drunk or injured, or taking over beside her when her driving freaks you out. Identify Bill.

9/12

You come home to a giant version of your old house, where you and your friends lived and partied. A huge tree grows through the middle of it. Sometimes your GF comes over and you two climb the tree together. Sometimes you just hang out by yourself in the tallest branches.

In the room across the hall, a half dozen people in various stages of undress sprawl on a big bed and nearby chairs. They are all napping, boys and girls together. You say, "Looks like a cuddle party."

You're conflicted. You'd like to join, but you don't want to sleep next to some stinky hippie dude. You feel like a square for being so hung up.

But your GF comes over, and the two of you cuddle in your own bed. You are naked together. She sits up on you with her hands on your chest. Over her shoulder, you see someone familiar in the room. "Is that my old friend from high school?" you ask. She says, "Yes, it is."

She is so beautiful. So beautiful and so sad at the same time.

Later that night, you visit your grandmother at her house. You're hungry, so you go into the kitchen to get some soup that's warming on the stove. It's a thick soup full of baked beans and mashed potatoes. At first it looks like a lot of food. But after a quick stirring, you eat it all in three or four bites. Strange!

You wash the dishes and clean the countertop. Look at how the towels are laid out just so on the countertop. How many years has grandmother had these towels arranged just like this? Is she lonely? Or obsessed? Or just particular? All three? You wonder just how much loneliness drives people to make pointlessly orderly arrangements over and over again.

9/16

You go to an outdoor concert and smoke pot at a table under a tent with your friends. There are chunks of pot everywhere, but you find a lot of grass and dirt in it. You clean it up and pass it to your friend.

In the DJ booth, another covered area in a tent, a guy sits down with a guitar and starts to sing the Butthole Surfers. "Julio Iglesias... Jacked off in outer space-ee-ass!"

It's the jam from *Hairway to Steven!* Some other people recognize it, and he receives thrilled applause. You are so excited you jump up and down with him yelling, "Julio Iglesias! JACKED OFF IN OUTER SPACE-EE-ASS!!"

The environment changes from a picnic so that the party now is a smaller gathering in a room containing the singer and the DJ. Everyone continues to dance, party, and rock the fuck out.

You go outside eventually. The Screaming Trees are throwing a spontaneous concert in the alley. They play some of their older numbers with an organ player, except it's the singer playing the organ. A bunch of black-wearing hipsters gather around them to listen. Your GF is with you. You take her up to meet the band after the show and say, "This is Mark Lanegan." Suddenly you realize these guys look nothing like Mark Lanegan and the Screaming Trees, which explains why the singer was playing the organ. Still, it was just as much fun as the real thing!

9/17

It's night, and you're driving the truck. Traffic is bad. You have to be careful about positioning your vehicle around all the other cars.

In the daytime, you ride your bike up to a comic shop. It's a bookstore with bookshelves and the comics are filed in with the books. The owner tells the customers that everything in his store is complete product, the original product, and the complete product, with all original materials. He has a book with a hard cover Jimi Hendrix comic book. He explains it has ALL the original material and is complete. You figure that means it has the original CD and the dust jacket.

You browse. Everything is in sections. Godzilla books are all together. You've never seen so many paperback novels about Godzilla. All the nature books are together. They are HUGE. The size of a kitchen table. Massive photo books. One has a picture of a tree on the cover. A big stump with gnarly root systems and burls. Other books feature animals.

They make you think about your GF for some reason. You remember you two used to read big picture books together, about nature and animals. This one about cats; you read it before together. Maybe you should get some of these giant books to read together.

The store even has a couple of life-size figures of Rorschach from *Watchmen*. Check him out. He was your favorite character of the series. The tag says $100 in large black marker on a white card.

You try to adjust a two-sided folding shelf. You get it all wrong, even though this girl tries to help you. You just want to make a small adjustment, but you do not at all comprehend the mechanism. You fold it up over yourself, get caught, and end up on your hands and knees on the carpet. You attempt several configurations before you manage to fold it into the shape of a chair with all of the books off it. It becomes a bench.

The girl seems pleased with the bench, and together you put a blanket and pillows on it. Now it's more like a futon bench. You make a little arrangement of mini-pillows on the arm of the couch but stop because you think you may be overdoing it. This chick is going to think you are a flamer, decorating with tiny pillows like that! But she thinks it's cute, and you sit together on it.

10/10

You and the GF are driving in the car. You are in the driver's seat. A two-lane highway takes you gliding alongside the coast. The ocean is on her side, though sometimes when you turn it looks like it's right in front of you.

You take the curve way too fast and slide into the other lane. You almost hit a wall of rock head-on. "Someday," you say to GF, "they are going to put me in prison for pulling this shit."

Suddenly you can see from a point outside of your body, over to the left and behind you, and you and your GF look like characters in a movie. Time slows down to slow motion.

You watch the car almost come back into a smooth trajectory, but it ends up dipping off the side of the road and flipping over. As it flips, GF is thrown out of her window and hits the beach.

You feel terrible for having caused this and hurt her. But you see it all from a distance.

Then you and she are together, unharmed, at a resort. The resort is expansive, containing a hotel, a bar, a restaurant, and administrative offices, all sprawling along a beach.

You go inside together and start looking around. You come to the end of a wing filled with offices. You feel hungry and broke. The two of you hope to find food and money.

GF says, "Watch this. Check this out." She goes into an empty office. When people come by, she pretends to be the girl who works there. Everyone calls her by her real name. She seems to have found an office with a girl with the same name as her! She fools everybody.

They all stop in to see her and sometimes they discuss whether it's really her or not. A few people think she looks different. But she sports a radically different haircut, punked out, spiky, multi-colored, and all the girls figure that explains it enough. "She got a haircut."

You get the impression she intends to take a lot of food and money out of the place. It seems dangerous, but you can handle it. It seems clever. You help yourself to a cup of coffee from the machine outside her office. A lady sits next to the machine.

Over the intercom comes the announcement: "A pair of guys is in the building masquerading as employees..." Interesting. A pair of guys. You say it out loud. The woman at the coffee machine fails to grow suspicious. Then the intercom again: "And a guy and a girl."

Oops. They're onto you! But who is the pair of guys pulling the same stunt you are?

You tell GF, "We need to leave." But she's sure she can pull this off. So sure that she refuses to leave when you do.

You take your cup of coffee and get the fuck out of the building in the fastest route you can find. You must climb over the edge of a balcony reserved for dining. At street level, you walk off quickly.

You see GF in the street with some guy. Who is that? Maybe it's one of the guys you heard about over the intercom.

Cobblestone streets.

A section of town that looks just like Europe. You meet GF and the guy on a college campus. He wants nothing to do with you. Maybe he's territorial about GF already. He says, "Don't you know who I am?" For a second he reminds you of your childhood friend. But that's not his face. Maybe it's Kevin.

You remind the guy of the time you punched Kevin for getting on your nerves. You say he had it coming. You and Kevin go back to the hotel, part of the administrative or residential complexes, and end up in a bathroom. It has a door to the outside, and outside is the beach.

You say, "Look, Kevin. I might have punched you when you wouldn't stop bugging me, but I was the only person who tried to be your friend. The others wanted nothing to do with you. They teased you all the time. I tried to be your friend."

A third guy appears in the bathroom. He just appears. He holds the door shut as if he's afraid of what's on the other side. He shouts a warning at you. The last minute of the scene is pure escalation of tension until... BOOM!

A loud noise jolts you awake. Like a cracking or splitting or a thunderclap. You sit up in bed, on edge and alert, looking around for the source of the noise. On your phone, you have a message from someone named Kevin.

This is the second dream where you and a friend encounter danger, flee, end up in a bathroom, and are wakened by a loud boom.

10/12

Marty's dead. You assume responsibility for the body. You wrap Marty in a blanket, one of those scratchy wool blankets people keep in their cars for emergencies. You scoop a little snow off the ground and put it in the blanket to preserve the body. It isn't exactly winter, and it's a sunny day.

Before you bury Marty, you stop at your GF's place. You sit down on her bed and talk with her. She tells you she had sex with a couple guys the night before. It was a group, with a bunch of different guys and girls. You mostly feel shock, followed by a little jealousy; then you let it go.

The two of you go out to your car. She says Marty has been in the car so long he's starting to stink. You can't smell it, but she does. You really need to get him buried soon.

You go and visit your friends. They want to discuss your GF's having sex with all these people again. "What the fuck is going on here?" you think. Marty's still wrapped in the blanket in the car.

Daredevil, the Man without Fear

You are Daredevil from Marvel Comics, the man without fear. Mostly the point of view is from your perspective, but sometimes you seem to be outside your body watching the action take place.

You find yourself inside a hallway, a stairwell, fighting ninja. You totally kick their asses. Your GF Karen Page is there. After the fight, you walk outside. It looks like a school. As you stand outside the door, you survey the ring of cops and people and cars waiting there for you. Are they here to support you, or just here to hassle you?

Internment Camp: Prisoners of Fear

In the internment camp, you all sleep in barracks and have routine duties. After many months there, you decide to take off. On one of your permitted trips on the bus into town, you decide not to go back. You wander into a subdivision in broad daylight looking for an abandoned house where you can hide out.

You find one and force the lock. Inside, you peel the black paper out of the living room windows to let in natural light. It's more dangerous to be exposed, but you crave the light and the feeling of openness.

Take a look around the house. Clear some old dinnerware way from a grate in the living room floor. Inside the grate you find food. The house is generally well-kept. You find some pot on the top of a bookshelf. You start breaking up the pot. Suddenly a guy and a girl show up. You know them from the internment camp. The three of you hang out, enjoying your taste of freedom.

Then another female shows up. She claims she is the owner of the house. You feel worried and embarrassed. You thought it was abandoned. But she's totally cool, and you all hang out together. She seems to support your escape, but in the end offers to drive you back to the camp so you don't get in trouble.

She takes a liking to you. She says to you, "Kiss for day?"

You say, "What?"

She repeats, "Kiss for a day?"

"Oh, sure!" you say, and share a little kiss. It's fun and exciting.

All four of you get in her big blue car. Everybody's in the car, but the chick from the camp is driving. Are you really going back? It reminds you of the story about the abducted woman that was forced to live in a box under some sicko's bed. They raped and tortured her for years. When they finally let her go to town, her mind was so broken that she didn't try to escape. She just went right back to them and her little box! Now that is fucked up.

You also begin to question if the female really owned that house, or if she was just trespassing too. Before you left, you noticed all the doors were wide open—not something a homeowner would allow before dark.

You become disappointed in yourself. How could you be such a tool to go back to the camp voluntarily? There was a moment on the back porch, when you had the place all to yourself, where you enjoyed the blissful sunlight and the peaceful respite of freedom.

Visiting Old Friends

You visit one of your old friends from grade school. The two of you sit in a living room that's exactly like your grandparents' house. All the books and knickknacks are the same. Same furniture. Same wallpaper.

You and your friend look through a publication from your old school. It contains a reference to sex in an article. "What is this doing in here?" you ask. "This is a publication for kids!"

His wife joins you in the living room, and the three of you watch some pornography together on the TV. Sometimes the point of view shifts so that the screen fills the entire field of vision, as if you are in the same room being filmed in the porno. The porno is a movie of female asses, undulating, well-tanned and well-oiled, with glistening drops of oil punctuating the sheen. Everything happens very slowly without rushing.

Then you're back in the living room with your friend and his wife. You are all just sitting there watching the TV. You feel like you are about to have an orgasm, and it embarrasses you. You bid them farewell and leave through the front door. Turning around, you see the outside is exactly like your grandparents' house.

Where's Mom?

You are in some farmhouse when it becomes clear that nobody knows where Mom is. You go looking for her. In the barn, a man from Mexico, one of the farmhands, goes climbing up the side of the barn. The wall is immense, maybe five stories high. He climbs a wooden ladder up to a loft he has at the top.

You stand in awe of this feat. He had no safety net. And it was a long way up. You feel kind of like an excited kid about it and get a sense that even though it's amazing, you could do it too.

Then you're in the kitchen. Your GF's cat shows up, and the two of you play on the floor. She is really cute. It makes you happy to pet her, like you're rolling.

Later, you and Dad sit in a room with separate desks and computers, watching funny videos and shooting the shit. It's a sunny afternoon, and bright everywhere except inside the barn.

11/22

You walk into a desert plain surrounded by mountains. Forests cover the mountains. You see other forests in the distance. You are looking for one of the Taiko ladies from Tucson. You come to a structure, a one-story building on the plain. One of the ladies is there, and she says the other lady is on the mountain.

She lives in the building. The front door is a garage door, and the interior is like a guest house conversion. It's small but cozy. The two of you recline on cushions on the floor. Your GF's cat walks in, and you pet him lovingly. He is thrilled and makes eyes at you and purrs. It's heavenly, like rolling.

11/28

Wandering in the forest, you find evidence that some guys attacked a girl out there. Some of the girl's things are at the site of a campfire. You go off into the woods and pick up their trail. It leads you to an abandoned building. Inside, it's trashed. It looks like vagrants have been using and abusing it for quite some time, for years.

There's an article of the girl's clothing, fresh and new, with a tag. Her name is on it. You try to read it but some of the letters are blurry. Looks like, "Queen, Young," or maybe, "Queen, Ann." They must have taken the girl here.

Suddenly, people come into the room.

Is it them?

Year Two

01/18

You and the girl from school sit on a bench together. The bench delineates three sides of a square, and is bordered by red curtains. People nearby are dressed festively. Not outlandishly, but definitely party style. Spirits are high.

Soon, she is going to take off her shirt. You are thrilled but try to remain calm and nonchalant on the surface. She takes off her shirt. No bra. You try not to stare, but she catches you stealing glances anyway.

3/1

You take a job in an accounting office. You think about how accountants might be good referral sources. A woman in the office meets your eyes and confirms this is true. You know it, though not a word is spoken. You know, you are really on to something here.

3/14

You find yourself in an historic apartment building, talking to your friend from school. You take out a pistol. Something is wrong with the set up. It won't fire. But then, you adjust it and put a bullet in your friend. You fire a second shot. You fire a third shot at the floor.

He's dead. You decide to leave, take the gun, and ditch it later. Before you leave, you go through the apartment and remove every scrap of paper with your name on it.

The next morning, two guys are talking to you in your

apartment in the same building. One asks you if "the kazoo" got to you before you left. You pretend not to know anything about it. They tell you your friend is dead.

You become upset, nauseated, and tearful. As you cry, they drape something over you. When you finally open your eyes, you are covered by a sheet that is floating in the air above you, not really attached to anything.

You haven't moved, but the scenery has changed. There's a nice old lady talking to you, comforting you about your friend. But you're outside in some other city, and it's raining.

Now you are genuinely sad. The rain comes down. Grey and gloomy. You wonder what to do. You have to somehow go about your business. The woman leaves. You are all alone.

04/15

On the way back from meeting with your client, you think about calling an old friend and asking him what the going rates are for the services you've been asked to provide. He's done it before, and would have some good input.

Then you're barreling down a country dirt road in a huge old pickup truck at a high speed and not exactly out of control but certainly not stopping or slowing down.

The truck leaps into the air to cross train tracks and sections of gravel. You pass an old farmer and plow into a cornfield, full of tall adult plants. A blue hound is in your path. It's scared. It's right in front of you. Somehow you avoid a collision, and the dog is safe.

The truck continues up a hill on the other side of the field and then back onto a road. You drive through a rural town until you come to a coastal city. You've driven through this city many times before, and it's familiar. A detour for road construction makes your journey longer. You seem to drive for hours through many small towns and cities.

Eventually you come to your communications instructor's house. Her husband is there, too. They have a table in the living room, a massage table. The blue hound is on it. It is still with you. Did it come along for the ride, or did someone deliver it to your teacher? You pet it. It's a well-behaved dog. You pet its fuzzy belly. Then it falls off the table.

Don't worry. The dog wasn't hurt. Communication has brought a potentially dangerous situation into a positive moment.

Then your GF shows up. The two of you are invited to spend the night. When you find the bathroom, it's huge. It is like the inside of a sleek, white spaceship. More like living quarters for interplanetary travel than a simple toilet. Perhaps this is the bathroom of the future.

As you urinate, the water in the bowl becomes reddish. You see you are pissing blood in your urine, heavily. Somehow, you can view your urethra through your penis. You see a blood clot there. You push as hard as you can. It burns! But the clot works its way out, and a stream of bloody urine follows it. There's no way you could be pissing for this long. It should have stopped by now.

Then you see a tiny creature swimming in your piss. You get him on your fingers in a globule of piss and blood. He squirms. Then you see more of them.

You start to itch. The things are crawling all over your body in greater and greater numbers. The more you take off, the more there are! It's maddening. Frightening. What are you going to tell everybody else? How are you going to deal with this?

4/26

You end up at the artist's place. He's there with some female. You discuss something. He's packing up and leaving? You should let him get to that.

You go into the bathroom to pee but there's a little monkey drowning in a pot of piss in the middle of the room. You decide to rescue him. He looks like he's dead, but maybe you can save him.

When you rinse him off, he revives! He is happy to get the pee out of his eyes. He rinses in cold water from the tap. He becomes more animated and begins to transform. His size, shape, texture, all transforming.

Then he seems very healthy, and for a second you wonder how you are going to get rid of him! Cute, but can you deal with it? Then he takes a shit. He propels shit from his big ugly monkey ass right onto the floor. And... oh! Another blast of shit!

You think, "Fuck, I don't need this monkey!"

Then you look again in your hand. The monkey has changed into a tiny model of the artist, but with green skin. And he's wearing a black outfit like a Jesuit priest. Or maybe Keanu in *Matrix 2*. Then he begins to look like the Green Goblin.

Suddenly you're back at the artist's place re-examining something important. The day you killed the baby bird. It must have been summer of 1996.

5/27

You go to a Guns and Roses concert, and all of your best

friends from high school are there. You hug all of them, or at least warm handshakes. The cutest girl gets a hand on her butt. She's wearing her old jacket. One of your friends doesn't feel like talking. Another one shouts, "Give him the love!"

The concert hall is like the Dr. Who ship. It's bigger on the inside than the outside, which is just some old house, and not a particularly nice one.

The concert's over. Everyone is welcome to stay, but the bar staff is going to clean up. People are on their hands and knees applying some kind of wood cleaner to the floors. You go outside to pee.

Some girl has to pee too, and the two of you decide to pee in an alley. She squats. Your penis looks small. She touches it. You wonder how you're going to get rid of her as you pee on some bushes.

5/27

You and your GF get into some really weird shit with another couple and a guy. They get these people from a dance club, and take one of them up to this room. There, they secure her in a chair, remove part of her skull, and fuck around with her brain.

It seems interesting, maybe even cool, until the guy in the other couple suggests doing the same with your GF. He seems pretty set on the idea, but you defy him. He looks tough, but so what? You begin to edge your GF out of the room, but he steps right in. You get in his face as he starts talking shit.

6/12

The morning starts off well, playing at the playground and playing video games at the arcade. Then you go room to room in a building with colorful misshapen rooms like a funhouse.

Later, you join a group of students at a round table inside a Walgreens drug store. The instructor asks if everyone brought Sprite for the experiment. He says it's okay if we didn't, because he's going to buy one of the super big bottles. One of the girls comments that if there's some left over, she will drink it. The instructor says that she always says that.

You listen to a Fugazi album on headphones and look at the CD liner notes. This is not an album they ever recorded! The images in the liner notes are strange semi-human creatures. They have head/arms/torsos that become large larvae or pupa bodies. They look like something Jim Starlin would draw, but they're painted. The colors are the same colors of the rooms you went to before.

6/20

In a college chemistry lab, you discuss with the other students a demonstration involving a bomb.

At the demonstration, you take a brush and paint a line on the ground. The line goes from a table to some brick steps in front of a campus building. A medium sized crowd gathers. The guy who had the idea is talking about something.

You leave one spot in the painted line open. The line must be broken, because it is the fuse. The break in the line guarantees it won't go off prematurely. The explosives are in a bucket on the table.

Finally, you're done! Someone lights the fuse. You grab your backpack and get the fuck out of there! As you walk away, you look back over your shoulder to see the explosion. It's a good sized explosion that spews rubble and smoke from the middle of the crowd. You hope no one identifies you!

That night, it rains. You make your way through a series of parking lots trying to avoid security. Some guards stop you, but they don't connect you with the bombing.

The next day, you go to gym class. You are outside by the bleachers on the track. The coach has a pile of arms and legs on the ground. They are the limbs blown off people in the explosion. They don't look mangled or bloody. They could be limbs from mannequins, or maybe even GI Joes.

The coach talks about how horrible the bombing was, and how several kids that survived it are missing limbs. By the end of the speech, you can see the coach is still standing but only has one leg and one arm. Was he damaged by the blast, or has he always been like that? Did you just not notice because of prosthetics? You feel bad that your bombing created all these amputees.

6/26

You are part of a group of people in a forest. All of you know that soon the lights and electric power will go out, leaving you in pitch black night. That's when the zombies will be menacing you.

One man produces a trunk. You open it to reveal only a blanket. But, under the blanket you find a shotgun. It comes in two parts, barrels and stock, that snap together quickly. Everyone wants one for themselves, but you only have four.

One of the men suggests that having us running around scared in the middle of the night with guns may just get us all shot. That makes sense to you. You give your gun to another man. It makes you feel weak, giving up the weapon; then again, you don't want to go around accidentally shooting your friends. And they're all as scared as you are.

You go for a walk. Soon, you come across a high ridge overlooking a field and more forest below. Following the ridge, it becomes clear that the "immense forest" in which your group hides is nothing but a small park next to a residential area. You can also see that the lack of electric power is limited only to that park.

Now it's not so frightening. You feel bad for your group. They are still back there, hiding, scared, as if the whole world lies in darkness. If they had simply kept walking in any one direction, they would have found their way out to a whole new set of circumstances.

Eventually, you make your way to the small city. You end up at a coffee shop.

You walk up the bricked streets to a gate. This is your customer's house, except it has transformed into a Spanish villa in the mountains. These mountains are the same mountains where the Taiko lady was. You sit at a table outdoors with your customer, who is quite hospitable.

But in the living room, more people enter, and you get into a disagreement with them. You get on your bike and leave. You zip over to your parents' house, which is a motel complex. Outside it's sunny and warm. Inside, Mom is making Christmas trees, small shiny metallic trees. It is her tradition. Your parents appear in their thirties.

You decide on a shower. You put on some music. It's on a cassette player in the middle of the floor. Press play and walk to the bathroom. Just as you worry that seeing you naked might shock your parents, you are standing fully clothed in the shower. The tub fills with water.

At first you have trouble hearing the music, but it's clearly Fugazi performing "Shut the Door." It sounds so awesome! Ian screams, "Have you ever been CRRRUUUUEELLL!" It's a bit much for your parents though, and they stop the music. You all hang out and look at Mom's little trees.

Then there's a tree, a real one, with presents under it. And a kitten inside a paper bag playing with another kitten who attacks the bag. They remind you of your GF's cats.

Later that night, on the back porch, you hang out with your old school friends. Inside the door, there's a wood shop where all the punks are hanging out. That skinhead with cerebral palsy is repairing the leather on an old pair of boots. He asks you to go on a mission. Sounds like one of those things that always go terribly, pointlessly wrong. You don't decide either way.

The next day, you walk the beach with your female friends. From the shoreline, a walkway extends through the water to a raised wooden platform. The walkway is just below the water so that when you walk on it, you appear to be walking on water. The platform is about ten feet up in the air, with railings all the way around. It's almost like a chunk of old bridge. A couple dozen people could fit on it.

About thirty feet from the platform, a tree grows out of the water. Large birds sit in it.

You look down from another even taller structure, a concrete building several stories high. You look down on the platform and the tree, the people below, the females walking across the submerged walkway to the beach. What a view!

7/4

In the parking lot of your high school, you sit in your car listening to music on a vintage cassette player. This is the same car Jim Morrison drives in *When You're Strange*. He was dead then.

You remember your best friend. He's somewhere in this lot. A car comes up behind you. You're parked in a lane that doesn't have room for them to go around, so you begin to move. But then you're ashamed, for moving so quickly for them, as if you were frightened.

You move forward and pull into the larger lot. It's got some cars in it, sports cars, pristine and shining in the sun. They sport racing stripes and appear expensive. One of your earliest friends comes up to you, racing on foot.

You look past him and see a brightly dressed clown surrounded by kids and a few parents. Your friend tells you the clown is here to visit all the dead kids in the parking lot. All the ones buried there.

Next you see out from inside the ground. You're underground like the dead kids. Your friend tells you that you live this life, but then you're dead and you just end up as clown shit.

7/5

The couch in your apartment has been replaced by an aquarium. Inside the tank, you keep a baby fox. You made it a little den inside the tank where it can hide under blankets.

There's a little section of the tank filled with water. You need to add a viscous, synthetic liquid additive. The bottle says to prevent any contact with your skin. You can't make out the ingredients, but one is silicate.

As luck would have it, you get some on your right arm and it begins to itch and burn.

Suddenly, a storm breaks out. This is no ordinary storm. It's a lightning storm, full of balls of plasma shooting rays, crackling in every direction. Giant, violent orbs of white lightning tinged all around with bright blue.

And it looks pretty damned awesome.

All the windows and doors are open. In fact, you don't even have doors in your doorways anymore. There isn't much rain, just this terrible lightning that strikes the building repeatedly, and everything nearby, the houses and trees and poles.

You stand at the back door. You can see the mountain from here. The orbs of plasma are very close, right above the parking lot striking at your doorways and windows. You move back from the doorway, aware of the danger, but also entranced and amazed at the spectacle. Then you remember the fox and worry about her safety.

7/7

You visit the dark-skinned man in his home. He mixes drinks for you two at his mini-bar between the kitchen and living room. His whole place is paneled in fake wood paneling. It seems to be a really big trailer.

After a drink, you take your powders back into the bedroom. You sit on the edge of the bed. There's a nightstand there with a little flame and bubbling water.

You take your powders and cook them up into some primo crack rocks and lay them on the table.

You go back out into the living for more drinks, but your dad knocks loudly on the door. The brown skinned man says he'll take care of it. You go hide in the bedroom and hope Dad doesn't find you.

Later, in a broken-down bathroom with a dirty mirror, you hear a voice tell you to make a video to apologize to your father. You have a stack of DVDs with you, including Clint Eastwood's *Dead Pool*. The voice tells you that to be effective the video must be honest and personal.

You begin to make the video... and then you're watching a guy play his video on a crappy little TV in the basement from the movie *Saw*. The guy in the video looks into a dirty toilet as his voiceover apologizes to his father. Even in the dream, you are embarrassed to see something so intimate and personal.

7/8

In an apartment complex in New Mexico, you find a boy growing a power outlet and propeller device out of the sidewalk. It shoots flaming jets of propane. It's pretty cool, if maybe a bit dangerous in the desert. The kid is having a great time with it.

Down at the end of the apartment row, in a dead end created by a fence, you can see another propane device. This one is blocked by some piece of metal crap, a busted old corner of a fire escape or something. You and the kid go to the end of the row to check it out. You see that if you screw the metal thing into the wall, where it has some holes that line up with holes in the building, you can access the propane thing. You and the kid get to work on affixing the metal to the wall.

You wake up in some house. Your GF and some guy are there. You go outside for a walk. Across the street, cops chase a kid. Then the kid gets a big white horse. He pulls some stunt where he leans over the side of the horse, almost touching the ground, escaping the bullets from the cops. Snow covers the ground. The kid wears his winter clothes. He is just inches from the snow, hanging from the saddle.

Later, at your car, you call director Ang Lee on the phone. He was the director of the whole street scene you just witnessed. He seems impressed you knew it was digitally manipulated. He explains how he edited out a bunch of leaves on the ground to put in the white snow.

After a little chat with Ang Lee, you hang up. You walk back to the trunk of the car and roll cigarettes on it.

7/13

You ride your bicycle through the woods for hours. Every so often, you see a house. Somewhere in the forest could be the neighborhood where you were a kid.

Eventually, you come to a clearing, a lot with a single wooden building built like a rest stop. One of your shoes gets stuck in the mud. You take your bike to the rim of this clearing, which is slightly higher ground. You turn to look back towards the missing shoe, but the lot is now covered in water. Maybe you can wade in the water and find it.

The water level rises. By the time you get to the spot where you lost your shoe, a strong current takes over. Just staying in place takes incredible exertion. A young man is out in the water. Who is he? He makes it to shore, and so do you, right behind him.

As you climb out of the water, though, you see the shoreline has changed. No longer dirt and rock, it becomes sculpted concrete. You find a handhold to pull yourself out into a new landscape.

You and the young man stand on a bridge. Concrete and cables stretch in both directions. In one direction, it leads to the city.

7/14

You and your GF swim in an indoor pool. She has a pet with her in the water, a miniature black seal. It swims with the two of you playfully then heads to the end of the pool.

The seal comes out of the water onto the ledge surrounding the pool, but it bumps its head. Is it hurt? No, it's fine. The seal lies on its side facing the pool, with its head tucked into the corner of the ledge and the wall.

Up to your waist in water, you stand and pet the seal. It has a short, soft coat of fur. It begins to purr as if it really likes you. The features begin to morph into the face and breasts of a plump young woman with dark skin and long black curls. You become happy and excited, petting the seal/woman. She says to you, "Suck my dick." And you say to her, "If you had one, I would suck it." So, you keep petting her quite happily, and soon her features morph back into a seal.

7/15

You are Spider-man, flying through the air, through the sky, above an ocean liner. People on the deck of the ship have a serious problem. Sections of the deck come apart, shaped like giant puzzle pieces, and stick to the people's shoes. The problem has to do with real estate. You shout down to them, and your words solve the problem.

8/30

You walk through the hallways of a university hospital, looking in doorways and windows, observing. Looking for something. You find a door that leads to a stairwell outside. The stairwell, a concrete hallway with steps and openings for windows but no panes, takes you up the side of the building to the rooftop.

Your GF is there with her best friend, discussing what happened to her orange cat. She says he "turned into something else back there." She doesn't know what, but it disturbed her. You have a vision of the cat in the hospital, but he's turned into a kind of shell or container holding strange organs and unusual permutations of flesh.

The vision ends, and the three of you find yourself walking along train tracks. You understand now what happened back there. The cat mutated into something else, and that something died or was killed. It makes you sad. You loved that cat, and now you'll never see him or hold him again.

9/13

You and your GF visit the house of an old friend of yours. The house is her house downstairs, but upstairs it's more like the house of an even older friend.

At the top of the stairs is an orange cat. Your friend needs to find a home for it. It's a really nice, mellow cat, purring as you pet it.

You ask how old it is. She tells you it is thirteen. "That's good," you say. You don't want to commit to a cat for a whole seventeen years, but three or four sounds about right.

Your GF comes over to see the cat.

9/24

You are in your childhood body, visiting a place from your childhood: a backyard with a clothesline and a small garden plot surrounded by tall grasses. Behind the lot is a house that looks like a church, with a small white cross at the peak of the roof.

Written on the house is a short religious slogan, along the lines of Thou Shalt Have Faith. As you read the slogan, you think about how your father never liked these people. He said they weren't real Christians like he was, and he's always had a beef with them.

9/24

You find yourself in a small space indoors, an enclosure you've created. The walls are all shelves, and they're all filled with comic books. This little room in the basement is very tall but barely wide enough to turn around in.

You sit on the floor, reclining, stretching out your legs. Despite the small area, you don't feel claustrophobic. In fact, you feel safe, secure, protected, comfortably enclosed. With a little library ladder, you can climb up and see out into the rest of the basement. It's dark and huge, but not scary. The welcome seclusion of a private space.

Later, you take a trip to another room, but this one is above ground floor. Massive windows span the length of the room, and you can see clouds. It's like a large penthouse.

You meet a guy who has a box of comic books to sell. One set of collected trade paperbacks he has looks really nice, and you want them. You say you value the whole set at $120, but he says it's probably closer to $15.

Now that's exciting! You are going to get a great deal! You look through the books some more.

10/2

Charlie finds a camping spot. You and two close friends drive through the woods on a two-lane paved road, past a bridge and a creek, and then get out. Later, you go for a solo drive.

Even later, you chat with Charlie on Facebook, thanking him for telling you about the place. You had such a good time there! But when you try to remember it, it's all fragmented. Like reading a book but skipping lots of pages.

That night, you're in bed with an older female acquaintance. You are sitting up in bed and talking, like a married couple might do, in your pajamas. She tells you that her husband might come home and see the two of you in bed and get the wrong idea. So, you get out of bed to dress more appropriately in case he comes back. He doesn't, and the woman keeps talking.

10/7

You make a connection with an illustrator for the comic book you are scripting. You work with him on a college campus, producing your book.

10/7

You sneak into a house that isn't yours. The owners are a black family, and you are black, too. You aren't there to steal anything, but you are definitely being covert about checking it out. Then, you see the owners are returning. You get spotted and become very anxious about getting away without any conflict.

10/9

Sitting across from someone else at a restaurant table, enjoying the brightly lit afternoon, you pick up a water jug from the table and start testing various spots for sounds. You tap on all the different surfaces, from different angles. In your hands, tucked against your body, the shape of the thing begins to transform. Soon it becomes finished ceramic pottery, glazed in green.

You begin playing it like a drum, percussively. It has grown a little mouth you can clap your hand over to make a deep bass sound, and you dig that. You realize you are *trying* to play the object when you should simply be *playing* it. You let go of conscious effort, of attempting, and just do.

12/13

Two snakes crawl out a canvas sack, grow in size, then slither down stone hallways. The stones are tight fitting cobblestones under vaulted ceilings supported by pillars.

As the snakes slither away, you remember all your previous dreams of snakes. Suddenly, you feel the continuity of years of dreams about the snakes. All the times they got out of control, filled the house, started biting people, and generally making trouble. They always seem to multiply at a rapid rate. They are aggressive but have incredible multi-colored designs unlike anything you've ever seen.

Now you recall all of that, and you hope this time the snakes behave themselves. They do, but they have no interest in being caught again. They slither off on their own.

Outside, the city is massive but empty, a giant stone city with no inhabitants. You view it from the rooftop. It goes on in every direction.

12/27

You and your friend are held prisoner by an alien in a condo set on the expansive greens of a large suburban golf course. The alien wears a string of lights on its head. You and your friend are not shocked or unsettled, and this seems to be a clue that the alien has mind control powers over the two of you.

You all sit at the dining room table until the alien gets up and walks down the hallway to its bedroom.

You sneak down the hallway to check it out. The alien stands, facing about 90% away from you. You and your friend decide that while the alien is in there preparing to communicate with other aliens, it will not be focusing its attention on you.

The two of you run out the side door, through the garage, and across the greens of the golf course. It's night, but a full moon gives light. Just when you feel home-free, the alien is there, in front of you, walking towards you! You run, but the alien gains on you. You turn a corner, but the alien is there already, walking towards you. The alien has another thrall in its mind control, and the four of you start to fight.

You try cutting the alien's throat with a beige plastic knife. It doesn't work. You are so frustrated and filled with rage! You want to kill this alien! You punch it and hit it as hard as you can. Your heart pounds in your chest.

12/29

You set up to do music at a public performance hosted by your public speaking instructor from college. You plan to do some improvisational jams and soundscapes, the kind of things you spent the year recording at home. It makes you excited and happy.

The performance takes place in a mostly outdoor courtyard of a multi-level building, not a skyscraper, but at least two levels. During your performance, a girl goes upstairs to answer a question. That level holds a library furnished in the style of a popular bookstore. You decide to go up there for a bit.

That's just one of many interruptions to the performance. In fact, you seem to spend more time being interrupted than actually playing music! But you get some of the jams recorded on your portable recorder. It crosses your mind that so many interruptions should bother you, but you feel alright about it anyway. You are just excited to listen to what you recorded, and you wrap up the show.

On the way home, you make a detour and ascend a set of stairs to an apartment. Your GF and some other chick are in there, all dolled up and making out. They invite you to have sex with the two of them.

But it isn't just you. Also present now is the guy you were with when you were fighting the alien before. Is he a part of you, or someone else, or perhaps the embodiment of how people see you? You are not sure. But you do know that before the two of you can have sex with these two chicks, there are some things you have to do first; namely, get something to eat, and listen to your recordings!

You leave and drive somewhere to pick up food then head back to your pad. Your apartment is decorated in a very modern style with an interesting staircase in it. You sit and listen to your recordings, feeling very excited about them.

12/30

You look at a letter from your aunt. It has an interesting photo of her, a close up of her face in profile so you can only see one eye and some of her hair. It seems more compositionally creative than most of the photos she takes. She has written some personal text to you in her letter and enclosed a few more pictures.

You read them in your office and place two of the pictures on your bookshelf, a picture of her daughter, and a picture of a moment from your childhood. The moment has great personal significance to you. There's an object on the ground...

You look at another picture that shows a girl you went to high school with. You wonder why your aunt would send a picture of someone you knew in high school. But as you look at it again, it transforms into a picture of your sister. She is smiling naturally, with dyed black hair and streaks of blond in it.

Maybe this is a magical picture that can create many moments and people from your life every time you look at it; in a sense, like the internet.

Year Three

You stand in a patch of big rocks on the edge of a small clearing with a large rock pile in the middle. It's high up in the air over a beach, although you can't see the beach or the cliff face from this vantage point. It reminds you of Patrick's Point or Trinidad.

On the left, the rocks form a semicircular border. Over this border charge Hannibal and his elephant. The terrain is difficult for the elephant. As they come charging down into the clearing, they pass the rock formation in the center and disappear.

In your left hand, you hold a button which you press. It is a reset button that resets Hannibal's charge. Here he comes again on the elephant... and there he goes!

You realize he isn't just disappearing. He and the elephant are falling off the edge of the cliff! You get a visual flash of the two of them falling to their deaths on the beach below. It's a long way down, so you push the button again... and there they go!

You wonder why they don't just slow down. The next time, it happens in slow motion. You see the elephant can't find its footing as it comes down the rock wall, which is why it has to run. It has no time to slow down before it hits the drop-off... And there they go again! Boom!

You push the button again. This is kind of fun! You are bringing the two of them back from the dead to do this charge over and over, a cosmic instant replay. You must go through it half a dozen times before you start to wonder if (A) they are ever going to notice, and (B) if you are really fucking up the space time continuum messing with it this way.

Sure enough, the next time around, Hannibal comes over the rocky barrier, his hair now a long, wild reddish color. He looks directly at you before he and the elephant go through their routine again. He may not know exactly what is going on, but he certainly suspects something. You have a sense that no one could die and be re-created that many times without beginning to realize it, going nuts, or both.

You find yourself sitting in a room with your sister, telling her about this dream. The room resembles your childhood bedroom in Long Lane, except the windows are placed differently. It seems connected to the larger house you have dreamed about repeatedly for the last couple of years, the giant house where all the rooms of the past and present are somewhat connected.

Briefly, you get a flash of the other rooms in the top of that house: the giant living room with the sunlit windows and huge couches, the parts not obviously connected to the lower floors, some of them versions of rooms from your childhood and some of them seemingly unique to the house. As you describe the dream to your sister, you point out that the clearing in which all the action took place was about the size of this room.

1/09

You visit a house with your high school friend and some other people, a huge estate with hills and forest and a swimming pool. You've been here before in another dream and played in the pool then. You make a phone call.

Then you're in bed with your GF, but she has black hair.

The room resembles your parents' room on Highview. You ask her, "If money was no object, where would you go?" But of course you know where: Hawaii.

She says, "Of course! And you?" You tell her you would leave in the afternoon to fly to a city with an art exhibit, stay overnight in a good hotel, see the exhibit the next afternoon, hang out, then come back the next afternoon.

1/11

You are in a house with Mom and Dad and maybe your sister. A man outside with a rifle plans to attack you. You crawl on the floors, avoiding windows. The man sent a message that we won't see it coming but he's going to kill us. The house has a lot of hiding spots: doors, windows, corners. You expect him to leap out of any one of them at any moment.

You frantically realize you can never cover all the possibilities. You don't even have a weapon! So, you grab a screwdriver. It seems small and pathetic against the danger you face, but it's all you have.

Suddenly the attacker is in the house. You grapple with him. You gain the upper hand, even though you're a kid and he's an adult. You try to drive the tip of the screwdriver into his throat. It is a desperate struggle. You are AMPED and TERRIFIED and nothing else in the world is more important than driving this goddamn screwdriver into his larynx or jugular.

Mom stands there with the guy's rifle. He laughs at you because you can't kill him. "MOM," you scream, "Kill him!" But she won't. You scream and scream, but she won't take action. You scream, "DAD! Kill Him!!" But Dad won't take action either.

You are so angry with them! Why won't they do something to end this threat?! He is here to kill you all, and you have to take him out! But Mom and Dad shake their heads. "We won't kill him." Fuck! It occurs to you that they suck like superheroes who won't kill the villain but just let him run free to continue ruining our lives.

Suddenly it's over and you're just angry with Mom and Dad. You throw some shit and break stuff and take a piss in the basement before going outside.

Outside, you have a friendly chat with some neighbors and their friends in the side yard, looking at the rows of apartments across the field of your back yards, lots of apartments going to the horizon.

1/18

It's just you and this other guy. He has dorky blonde hair, a kind of bowl cut with a part, and a tweed jacket. You know him from somewhere. He tries to get you up from the couch, but you resist. You use one hand to hold on to the couch and grapple with him with the other hand. It isn't violent, just playful and silly.

For a moment, you see the whole scene as if a child drew it. You feel loose and sloppy, like you're drunk. Finally, you get off the couch to see something he wants to show you.

He shows you a large box in the next room, the living room, by the door. You could fit inside the box it's so big. He sits at the dining room table in the front room, out of sight but within conversational range.

You open the box. It's full of *Star Wars* toys, still in the original packaging. They're larger than any produced in real life. They look expensive, and there are a lot of them.

It's a nice gift even if you don't really have much interest or need for all these X-wing fighters and so on.

Then you notice there's a short box of comic books, bagged and boarded. You flip through them. Now *this* floats your boat. They're all in superb condition and grouped together, some early *Micronauts*, *Spider-man*, and so on, all of which have never been printed. Your brain is making these covers up just for the dream.

You're thrilled. But, as you discuss them with the guy, you don't know how you're going to take them all with you "when you go back." How will they fit in the car with all your other stuff? Do you have room in the trunk? Can you ship the spaceships and bring the books in the car with you? You thank the guy and chat some more.

2/4

On the phone with the GF at night in some house. You're on the first floor or basement level in a bed which is very close the ceiling, like the top of a bunk bed. You talk about ordinary things: how it's almost time for financial aid disbursements and you have no money.

2/4

You sit with your GF at an outdoor table at the Biltmore one night. She dyed her hair and styled it into a black bob. She wears a red t-shirt and blue denim jacket.

You tell her how you wouldn't lump her into any of the identifiable groups or types of people in the café behind you, where you got your drinks. "Not the rockers," you say, "although normally I would, and not the..." and so on. Your point is, whether you're making it clear or not, is that she is unique. She listens and nods, not saying much. Then the two of you get up and go to a club a few doors down where a band she likes will play.

She gestures with her eyes at your water, a cue that you should give it to a friend of hers at the next table. Instead, you drink the whole glass before realizing what she means. So you take her friend another glass of the water from your table. Except, when you give it her, it's obvious you drank most of it, too. Lip prints all over it. Fingerprints all over it. Not very smooth!

Then you and your GF go into the club. You breeze past the door and don't pay. You stop at the men's' room just inside the door. Inside the urinal stall is another super tiny room with nothing but a sink. You wonder if anyone ever just shit in the sink. You imagine a game in which you're playing "I Never," and your line is, "I Never shit in a sink."

2/6

You're hanging out at a party at the gallery. A fence stretches around the side where you talk to a security guard. At your request, he gets you a cup of coffee and the two of you have a nice chat over the fence. He even gets you a refill. He asks how the coffee is, and you say you like it.

It's great to have a cup of coffee, even though you don't actually like the taste of this coffee. It tastes like Denny's coffee, or something you'd get at a gas station. But hey, it's a hot cup of coffee, and you like that!

2/11

In the living room with your family. You stand up and tell

your grandfather he's old and doesn't know what's going on. Not only is it disrespectful, but it also comes out a lot worse than you intended. You immediately apologize. Soften it by saying you're sorry. You were just joking. Then you hug him, nuzzling and snuggling him.

The entire scene fades away. The entire realm of existence condenses to the feeling of a loving snuggle: no people, no visuals, just a feeling.

Normally Marvel's "Essential" trade paperback collections print in black and white. You find one in color full of Spider-man stories. One of them is that John Romita, Jr. story about Ben Reilly in the rain.

2/13

In the room upstairs, in the dark, at a big executive desk in front of black curtains. You face a computer. Tonight, you're in the White House on a mission to change something on this computer. Your GF is there, off camera. A camera monitors the monitor, recording that you're there.

It concerns you for second, but fuck it. By the time security gets this footage, you'll be gone. The pictures on the screen distract you, mesmerizing you for a moment. Pictures of you and your GF on a tropical beach. Gidget the dog is there. Hey, these are pictures you don't have at home. You take a minute to make copies of them.

Mission accomplished. Exit the room and go downstairs to get out. You take the stairs, a wooden two-level affair with a landing. On the way down, you see someone on the first level. Slip into a dark room, a kitchen at the end of the stairs. You turn around to sneak back up the stairs, but you are spotted! It's the guy from the gallery!

You do a back flip, hands on the rails, the entire camera angle rotating around you in slow motion from your point of view. You land, saying "Hey!" Guess what he wants to talk about... the website. Fuck.

So, you sit down at a table with him and discuss what he needs and wants. You tell him WordPress can do all the things he needs or wants. Everything he brings up, you just keep writing it down. "Okay, you want this? WordPress can do this!" Making big bold checkmarks on the page. "So what is the problem?" you ask him. You are patient, but it's just so damned frustrating.

2/18

You work at Target, stocking shelves. There's a product, a box that keeps popping up at the end of a row. It just appears then disappears. A manager walks by and sees it happen. It shocks him, but he remains casual, friendly, cheerful.

You tell him your belief that it's a ghost in the store, but he's skeptical. Eventually, he comes around to your way of thinking when it happens right before his eyes.

Then you both go about your business. Someone else comes over to see it. Eventually the shift ends and a manager walks by to his office. You follow. You both stand by the large window behind his desk, talking about going home. He says, no, they need you until 8:00 p.m.

"What? It's 7 a.m. and I've been here since 11 p.m. last night!" He acts like it can't be helped. But he smiles, and you're friendly. He's just busting your chops.

He chomps on some food and says, "Hey, what about me?" He's just giving you a hard time.

It turns out the two of you went to high school together

and were both in Earth Club.

2/21

You and your GF drive up to an outdoor park and fun house. It has a slide inside, a series of plastic tubes leading to the outdoors where you park. It reminds you of the Magic House in St Louis. The two of you want to get inside to ride the slide.

You arrive at night, but the sun rises, and day becomes progressively lighter. Behind the slide lies an open pavilion covered with caution tape. Some kind of cops or hired security show up and talk to you.

Elsewhere in the park, a long wall composed of nothing but glass panes. Windows. On the inside of the wall, an office. Animal cages. Different animals on the desktops. One of the windows is open so you and your GF can just reach in and touch them.

Now she's got one of the animals, a black kitten. She holds the kitten as a black raptor dive bombs them from the sky. He thinks the kitten is food.

You yell, "He wants that kitten!"

She yells, "I know," seemingly undaunted, protecting the kitten from repeated raptor attacks.

A new section of the park appears. As you walk around, it seems like a museum but one of those tourist stops: a "point of interest." You walk around and find what appears to be a pair of raptors. They are the size of humans, engaged in a flowing dance together. The splendor of this event stops you in your tracks to gaze in awe.

Suddenly, one of them breaks away. Now, it doesn't seem like a bird anymore but instead a park warden. Now you feel foolish. What you thought was two birds in a magical dance is just a couple of people from park security. You apologize for staring at them. You walk away, down a path around the side of the building, saying, "I'm sorry, but I just had a mystical experience."

You have two conflicting feelings simultaneously. One of awe and wonder at the mystical experience of the raptor dance, and then a feeling of embarrassment that it was only some mundane thing you were "really" seeing.

But isn't life like that? The sacred and the mundane, two sides of the same coin. All the shit we go through in life also has a magical, unconscious component charged with archetypal energy.

2/21

In a large garage or hangar, you and some other people prepare for a boat race. You can't shake the feeling that all of you will get lost on this journey and will not make it back, and a sense that the dream is re-living a story whose ending is already known.

On the boat, a thick fog envelops everything. Everything. Your entire field of vision nothing but a dense impenetrable gray. Someone next to you tries to see through the fog with you.

And then, as if you see it through a window or picture frame, you see the moonlight. The moon appears above a gigantic gray wave in a torrent of gray rain from the sky, and the wave seems to reach as high as the moon. This striking, powerful image fills you with a sense of terrible awe and wonderful fear.

Soon, you see another boat slip past in the fog, so silent it's scary. Then, the fog parts so you see an island in the night. People on the boat begin talking about the island.

Again, it fills you with a sense of simultaneous beauty and fear in a terrible inspiring way.

It may not be such a good idea to go to the island. Something bad might happen. Of course, you already know everyone gets lost on this trip and does not make it back. More boats slip silently by in the night. They seem to come from the island, tainted with a ghostly evil and beauty. You think of them as cutters, although that may not be nautically correct. Not ships, not yachts, but some sort of long boat.

You think, "If we get lost, we can just turn around and head back towards the island." But you fear the island, and you know you all get lost anyway, never finding land.

The boat contains an interior as big as a house with a full kitchen and living room and people on the couch. Later, you're inside, trying to make a repair to a broken mechanism. You say to the others, "If we get lost, I'll wish I hadn't used all these up." But you know that's ridiculous, because you already know you all get lost.

Later, you attend a trial concerning what went wrong at the boat race. A judge presides. An effeminate man asks questions of the judge from the audience, like, "Don't we have to apply the question, 'If they hadn't done what they did, would tomorrow have still come?'" He seems to imply it was necessary to do what you all did on the boat, as if you ate the crew or killed someone, none of which you remember actually happening on the boat.

A man helps someone unload some stuff from the back of a hatchback car. You realize you've seen him before, loading something before the boat race. It's a clue to what went wrong on the boat during the race, the key to this whole damn trial.

The dream becomes more disjointed around a big

reveal that the guy in the yellow coat is the woman's son! So you follow them, the guy and the woman, and there he is, helping her unload the car! They are parked at a building with a layout similar to your apartment. The guy has a door where your door is, and the woman has a door next door or two doors down. She's some kind of Latina, Brazilian perhaps.

The yellow coat guy and the woman transform into a slightly different woman and her daughter. The daughter's name is Lydia, and her mother is going on and on about what Lydia's going to be some day. She talks incessantly about how Lydia will be a go-go girl. It's hard for you to tell if Lydia really wants to be a go-go girl, because her Mom never shuts the fuck up about it. You're all inside an apartment building decorated in Victorian style or something out of the *Amadeus* movie.

Finally, you return to the outdoor venue where the trial was held. The woman has changed from Brazilian to Jewish with a different look and different voice, still going on about the go-go girl debate and Lydia. You have no idea what it's all about, but the images of the moon and the wave and the dark island and the ghostly cutters stay with you even after you wake up.

2/23

You're at the high school reunion talking to a girl you had a crush on in grade school. The two of you discuss how you thought you'd marry her someday, and then talk about how her and her husband ended up getting married.

2/25

Driving at night, you stop into a small shop in the boonies. They have a problem with a dangerous individual. You go into the back room, taking your frog with you. Both of you wear brown law enforcement uniforms like state troopers or sheriffs. Your frog wears a wide-brimmed hat and is the size of a human.

The two of you look at the walls and ceilings of the room, which are coated in leafy vines. The troublemaker hides in there, but you can't see him. Your frog says, "It's a bear." You can't really make out the bear, but the frog is convinced.

Then, you're looking down into a glass bowl and both of your frogs swim there, at normal size. Suddenly, one of them gets sucked downward and vanishes. The other frog tells you, "It's the bear! The bear got him!"

You think, "How the hell can the bear be invisible and at the bottom of this glass bowl?" You worry. You don't want both frogs dying, so you scoop the last frog out gently into your hand and carefully exit this weird room.

But, when you get back into the main store, you are stunned to see a bear in the clothing of the woman who was at the counter before. The bear has killed her, eaten her, and donned her clothing!

Then, you realize the bear is actually a cute black bear, but it killed the lady at the store and your frog. It wears a bright yellow jacket. You grab an axe and bludgeon the bear to death until you are not angry about your frog anymore.

2/25

Walking through a city at night, making your way back to your hotel. The city appears somewhat futuristic but not overly so.

Then you're in India, visiting a huge estate. You walk along train tracks to a bridge. India sure is beautiful, not dirty and smelly like you heard about. You walk with a guy and a girl. They are brother and sister. You stand by the river, near a bridge, talking to the guy.

2/25

You travel to a village in Africa. You're with a group of villagers and travelers, some of whom are in your family. You walk through tall grasses on an expedition. The people of the village are not well. Something is making them sick.

An old guy right next to you dies as you sit on the dirt floor of his hut. A cow in the hut starts spazzing out, rolling back and forth, kicking. You back against the wall of the hut to avoid the hooves. These are the final death throes of the cow.

Suddenly, it's time to leave. You all have to catch a plane in fifty minutes and must hike through the tall grasses to do it. You try to cram all your shit into a backpack, but it takes too long and doesn't go well. Then you remember your little black bag of toiletries.

Next, Dad stands there watching all this and mentions that you also have your guitar. Fuck! You have to lug that heavy guitar case through the grasses to the airport.

2/25

With your family, you are in a house composed of various houses you lived in during your life. The room you are in belongs to your friend. You are getting ready to leave, when you stop to look at some action figures he has on top of his pile of books, bags, and video games.

He has some sweet *Tron* figures, the red ones you used to have. You want to take them. You wonder why you consider stealing them instead of just asking if you can have them. He has some other cool figures, including one amazing version of a figure you once made out of Hammerhead from *Star Wars*: a shiny, glittery, jewel-faced alteration of the figure. It isn't the figure you made, because the knee joints are not double jointed like the ones you made. But it is well-made, and you want to take it, too.

2/25

You park your car and walk through a neighborhood full of empty lots and homes under construction. You stand and stare at one really big house, thinking you wouldn't want to live in it because it's too damn big. You walk by a similar house with a small sign in the yard displaying a price of $429K. Yeah right, you can't afford that.

Then you hear woman's voice. She stands in the middle of a nearby lot announcing the deals she can get for you on these houses. She says she can get you into the $429K place for $180 per month.

You're like, no way. It's two stories, tons of rooms. No way. You call out to her, "Did you say $180 per month?"

She says, "That's right!" So you start thinking, well, maybe you could do it after all. The price is way too high, but the monthly payment would be easy.

You walk down the street and pass an even bigger house. It has much more attractive architecture, looking more like a museum made of marble than a house. The garage has no door on it but a huge, vaulted ceiling and a cavernous room. It must be three or four stories high. How big is it inside? How many rooms?

Then, you picture in your mind the house that recurs in your dreams, how many rooms it has, and how cool it is that you can only access some rooms by teleportation. You probably haven't even seen all the rooms yet, and sometimes they change. Now why would you want to sink your money, effort, and time into one of these huge houses when you already have something even more amazing in your dreams?

The weather is funny. When you're looking at this house, it's bright and sunny. But as you walk around other parts of the neighborhood, it's grey and overcast, or raining. It rains as you walk back to the back corner of a row of houses. The ones on the end are apartments. Two kids play in the rain.

You remember you need to write down the dreams you have. In your waking life, you had not yet written down the dream about the bear and the frogs and the one about Africa, only thought about them.

When you go back to your car, it seems more like a buggy with no horses, or a wooden cart. As the kids play and it continues to rain, you take out a wooden tablet and carve on it with a knife or pointed utensil:

1: AFRICA.

Then you try to write FROG but you spell it:

2: FERG.

You wonder, "Why am I writing 'Fergie?'" As you start

to complete the I and E, you wake up.

2/26

You're talking to your GF in your kitchen. She stopped by with some hot food and wants to know what you've been up to. You recall that your last GF had visited you and brought her brother and best friend. You had to make some sleeping arrangements for everyone that didn't involve you and her in the same bed.

You walk to the bathroom and notice she left you a figurine of a grey Siamese cat that hangs on the wall, and it looks just like your GF's cat. Does it mean, "Think of me even though I've been replaced?" You realize she replaced a black cat that was hanging there before.

When you open the box of your GF's food, you expect gyros. But it isn't gyros, and you're disappointed.

You want gyros.

3/2

You meet with some people outside on a patio at a restaurant or resort. It's light out. You stop to play with a flashlight with a cat that's on the patio. The cat resembles your GF's cat even though the coloration is slightly different. The two of you play with the flashlight like a laser pointer. It is a happy time, playing with the cat. You think about how you like cats more than people.

3/8

Nature, fields, forests, rocks, and rivers. Your best friends from high school are there with you. You travel through several different locations, all immensely enjoyable and absorbing, visually and experientially rich.

3/19

You sit at a desk as if in a classroom. On the desk is a picture of a man in an ad on newsprint, in a paper about the size of the *New York Times*. The ad is the lower half of the right-hand page. You trace his features with an ink pen.

You look up to see a girl with white or bleached punky hair. There's something about her that seems linked to this picture. The man in the picture is an adventurer or outlaw in his 40s or 50s.

Next, you observe this same girl up against a refrigerator in an apartment. A guy kisses her ardently, moving against her. Both of them have their pants down and their shirts raised a little.

The guy is the adventurer, and the girl is the same girl from earlier, but they both look slightly different. Sometimes, your point of view shifts from being outside watching them to looking out from the guy's point of view, as if you are sometimes him and sometimes only watching him. Are you the aging sexual adventurer?

It reminds you of the scene from *League of Extraordinary Gentlemen* with Alan Quatermain and Mirna in the forest.

3/20

This chick from the bar is driving and you're the passenger. Another girl is with you. You stop in a driveway, maybe the other girl's house. It's light out. You get into the front seat, but the bar chick says your car is underwater, so she can't take you to your car. But she'll take you home so you can call AAA the next day to pull your car out of the water.

This ignites a flash of a memory: It's night, and you're driving your Grand Am around a curve at night when you run into this huge pile of tree branches in the road. The car launches into the air and down into this watery area which seems like the result of a flood rather than what's normally there.

The car begins to submerge, although it seems the tires make contact with the ground beneath the water. The car moves forward into deeper waters. It doesn't seem so deep that you couldn't get out.

Then, you're outside the car and fully underwater, with your feet on the ground below the water, holding your breath. It's dark and muddy. You feel the water on your face. You try to pick up the car and back it out to where it left the road. You have your arm through the driver's side window, shouldering the weight. You get it moving, but progress stalls.

Then you snap back to being in the car with the bar chick, trying to convince her of the importance of dealing with this now. The car has to get out of the water now because... "Because it's my car," you say, which even strikes you in the dream as rather inarticulate reasoning.

The other girl interjects an attempt to be helpful, but it's totally irrelevant. You tell her to be quiet. The bar chick says there's nothing we can do now about the car. You're stuck in the mud with no immediate solution.

3/20

Driving through hilly, forested scenery. You stop at a wooden building with glass windows and a peaked roof. It reminds you of the place where you and the frog detective encountered the bear. You stop there for a while, having dinner.

Later, you're on a balcony of a hotel in a small town, near a minor road with lots of one-story cheap buildings. Businesses and stuff, your typical junk Midwestern city. You smoke a cigarette, one of the first times you recall smoking in a dream.

You go downstairs to ground level and over to another apartment. The entrance is below a stairwell, shaded. A table and chairs sit in front of the living room window on the porch, next to the door. The stucco walls remind you of your first apartment in Vegas. You sit outside and smoke at the table. The tabletop is glass.

At another apartment, you stand on the ground floor looking up into a second-story window in the building across from you, across a parking lot. The window is lit. A person is inside. His lawn is transformed into the University of Michigan campus and all the colors transform into autumn colors, only brighter, like a saturated photo.

In the parking lot, your friend waxes his car. You grab a rag and stand beside him, waxing the car together. He tells you he doesn't need help but it's cool if you want to. Then he leaves. You wax a different car now, within eyesight of him. You polish the mirror around the driver side door. This car is your Grand Am, the same one that was underwater last night! Your friend drives off in his car. You polish yours in the parking lot as the sun sets.

3/22

Your mind keeps producing these dreams where you seem

to be assembling pieces of some project, synthesizing disparate parts into a whole. In one of the sequences, you are assembling images. Every time you fit two pieces together, they release bursts of light and energy.

3/26

You dream your GF is on the couch with some guy from the bar, in a house that isn't any house from waking life. She says she started sleeping with him a week ago, even though he's married. You kick him out and argue vehemently with her.

Next, you dream you and your high school buddies are being berated and yelled at by a guy who is a lot like the drill sergeant in *Full Metal Jacket*. You hate him. Finally, you've had enough. You follow him into the other room. He kneels at a large, low table in front of a sectional couch. The table surface is unusual, recessed and filled with some water in which a lot of little objects sit.

You grab his head, shove it into the water, and hold him down for all you're worth. As he struggles, you climb on top of him and plant your knees in the back of his head. You have no doubt about his physical superiority, knowing it will take all your strength to hold him down until he drowns. One of your friends helps out by restricting his movements from behind. Finally, he stops moving. He's dead.

To dispose of the body, you and your friends cut it up and put the pieces in plastic garbage bags. You cut off his head. You notice very little blood, and that the head is almost artificial: abstract shapes, cloth texture, like a dummy. Your friends stand by the door as you pick up the bags. It's a heavy load but you tell them, "I got it!"

Outside, you find yourself in a super-massive apartment complex, like it's a section of the city. The buildings stand five, six, seven, eight stories high, with people everywhere. To your left, a disturbance breaks out.

Cops and ambulances everywhere. The cop uniforms look like Steve Rude's uniform designs for cops on Ylum. One stands right in front of you. You walk past him in broad daylight carrying the body in the bags.

Fortunately, everyone is more concerned about the trouble in the other building. You walk by as if nothing is amiss, find an open dumpster, and toss in the bag with the head. You look for a separate dumpster for the rest of the pieces, but they're all piled full of trash. You don't want the stuff sitting on top of a pile where it might fall out into the street.

You end up throwing everything in the same dumpster, the only one that's practically empty. You fear they will sit there too long and start to stink, alerting the authorities of the dead body. You keep thinking you read a newspaper article about that somewhere.

On the way back, you see a couple guys from school hitting golf balls into a courtyard from a perch on a wall. You talk to them for a while. You go inside an empty, abandoned room. It's creepy, but you look around, curious.

Later, you and your best friend go into a room in another building. There's a girl on a bed, fully clothed. You and your friend start making up shit to talk about with her, with really no point other than an excuse to talk to her. You talk about boots, chicks' boots.

Out the window, you see you're in one of the many residential buildings, many stories off the ground, on a sunny day. It's a cheery, upscale version of the neighborhood from the previous sequence.

Then, another friend begins strumming a guitar and singing a song. You and your best friend converse about someone's emotional state or pain being the result of coming from a broken home. You suggest an answer, but the discussion ends.

3/28

You get an email from a customer inviting you to an event with entertainment plus dinner. The emcee's name is familiar, a guy who emcees events you've attended recently.

You show up and go into a room filled with chairs, benches along the wall, and a slightly raised stage platform at one end. The first thing you're asked to do is some kind of Catholic prayer. You and the people there say something and move to a second seating area, elevated beside the first.

This display of religion disgusts you. You protest by walking up and saying, "Forgive me, father," skip the rest, and walk off. Then you turn back and say, "Oh yeah, and forgive me, Mother, too." Were you making a point that god could be a goddess? You walk out.

Out the back door of the room is a large sunlit yard. It's a beautiful day, and you walk towards another building on your left. You see your talkative neighbor going the other direction but avoid him so he won't talk your ear off about nothing.

Soon, you enter the building, a kind of geodesic dome. The inside has restaurant-style seating and a large open kitchen in an industrial style, with stainless steel everywhere. It's surrounded by a stainless steel bar and a line of round bar stools. The cook reminds you of your friend.

You see some people you recognize and say, "Hey, is there where the Lancers are meeting?" Some don't recognize you, so you start identifying them, chatting with them. More come in. Pretty soon, the place seems full, and everyone is drinking, eating, talking.

3/28

You're with two chicks in a living room with art on the walls. One lives with you there, and one is visiting. The visitor realizes you made one of the pieces and asks if they are all yours. Some of them are not, so you say it will be easier to tell which ones you did not make. You start telling her about the artists behind the pieces.

3/28

You look at a shelf of dinosaur sculptures and toys. You talk with someone about whether or not certain sculpted dinos could fight the sculpted T. Rex and win. You point out one of the dinos and say that four of him could beat one T. Rex. You're also confident that two hungry Allosaurs could take him.

3/29

An imaginary Vietnam whose landscape resembles the Midwest. Is this your personal *Apocalypse Now*? There's no mission to kill Kurtz.

At night, by a lake, you and many people party on the back porch of a house. You are all part of a US military group. Something's wrong with the Captain. He takes a canoe out on the water by himself. Everyone worries he might kill himself. You have a talk with him.

Next, the group tubes and canoes down a river in bright daylight. It's Vietnam but looks a lot like Missouri. You come upon a cage built into the side of a riverbank.

You are in a small canyon or ravine below shore level. Hills line each side of the river, covered in trees and plants, giant trees not ancient but old. Built into the sides of these walls is a cage that protrudes over the river by about five feet, and above your heads. It contains three sub-cages, each with a mostly naked female. The females wear some adornment, feathers, bone necklaces, bracelets. They're not gorgeous but reasonably sexy.

You and the guys converse, then you climb up a ladder. The whole cage set up is like sticks and poles tied together with rope or gut at the joints and intersections. You check out the chicks. You brush the hair on one female's mound with the back of your finger. You see it in close-up. The lighting changes to dusk.

Night comes. You and the group hang out on a porch with a big deck overlooking a forest like where you used to work summers in Michigan. You and the Captain kick back in a pair of large wooden chairs, drinks in hand.

Three chicks come up to you. Two hover around him and one walks over to you. You check her out, size up her sexual desirability, and comment to the Captain. She is sexually available to you if you want it, and you are deciding on that.

The next afternoon, you and the Captain dress in casual camping gear and backpacks. You walk along a sidewalk beside apartments. The apartments are laid out like your GF's, with overhanging walkways on the second floor, support posts, lawn, stairwells.

The two of you enter an apartment. Who does it belong to? What are we talking about? Then you both leave.

Identify the Captain. He seems like an ally.

3/31

You notice some people from high school in a grocery store. They don't seem to know you, but you walk over and introduce yourself to an old schoolmate in the produce section. He looks at vegetables, but doesn't seem to recognize you. He shows zero enthusiasm.

Eventually, you walk outside. It's night, and you are in the parking lot, but all the subsequent scenes take place in broad daylight.

You stand by a car with your sister, trying to change a tire on a car. The dark-skinned man walks up in expensive clothes: dress slacks, shiny watch, an expensive Polo. He carries a truncheon or billy club with a small handle on it which sticks out at a right angle. He seems threatening, so you tell him to go away.

He swings the club at you. You decide to fight. He hits you with the club as you move in. You fall. You get back up and get in close to him. You pull him to the ground and sit on his back with your knees pressed into his back, doing everything you can to smash his face into the pavement.

He stops moving. You pick up an implement, like a shovel blade. His head no longer looks like a human head but some other material. You take the shovel blade and, with considerable effort, chop through his neck. Now it's time to dispose of the body.

At the edge of the parking lot lies an opening to a creek surrounded by fence and rocks. It reminds you of the creeks in Ballwin when you were a kid. In some weird dream topography, the creek runs a couple of stories below the parking lot. You throw the head and body down there.

You worry they will smell when decomposing, leading someone to discover them and trace the murder to you. Well, there's nothing to do about it now. The deed is done. You walk back to the car. Rather than being troubled by the event, you feel happy to have won the fight and got rid of the guy.

Time to move on.

4/6

A wedding takes place in the building you are in. At ground level, a hallway has an open entrance to the street. Outside, sunlight shines down on an urban environment.

Off the hallway lies an elaborate wedding chapel. It reminds you of the location of your aunt's wedding in the late 1970s. People fill the hallway and the chapel. Your father delivers a sermon. He makes a point about people going to hell and not having any choice in their lives. It seems out of place at a wedding.

At the other end of the hallway sits a staircase. You go upstairs to bathe. In the many available bathrooms, something is wrong with every tub and shower stall. Broken doors. An electronics panel that adjusts temperature is broken. Nothing fucking works.

You leave.

4/6

The owner of the bar talks to you one night about the shopping center building he just bought. He painted everything white on the outside except the frames and windows. He says several times that he bought the whole building so no one else could tell him how to paint it.

It does look a little weird. You see splatters on the frames and windows and think critically about what a sloppy job it is. No one else is around, just the two of you standing across a small strip of parking lot from the building, talking.

4/7

You dream about a library that feels a lot like the one where you worked as a teenager, despite looking nothing like it. You remember being there in another dream, looking at seriously oversized books on reading stands.

Tonight, you wander several floors of this library, rows and rows of stacks and shelves. Parts are dimly lit. Some just go on endlessly in every visible direction. Others have windows that establish boundaries.

You see your friend not once but many times. Every time he appears, he looks different. Once, like in early high school. Once with a beard, looking older. You get recurring glimpses of him in what seem to be different stages of his life, but he never speaks.

Then you're face to face with another friend, looking through a set of books from opposite sides of a shelf, then face to face with no barrier. You talk about something very seriously for a while.

Then, he gives a warning, motioning with his eyes and a slight nod over your left shoulder. You turn to see a third friend there, with a very serious look on his face. He says something loudly and sternly, perhaps an angry, inflammatory profanity.

The second friend goes quickly out the door, as if he

expects the shit to hit the fan now. The library staff shows signs of being upset. They want to take some action against the third friend, and you know he won't go without a fight.

Why is everybody so serious?

4/12

You and a bunch of guys in brown suits are in a brown room. Everything is shades of brown except their black ties and your black leather jacket. You give them a consultation, but it feels more like an interrogation, like you're in trouble.

You tell the guys after you make your statement about your findings that you don't think going to war is a good idea. But, considering what they are willing and unwilling to do, going to war is probably the only choice for them.

You gather your things, your black binder and some papers and files, and exit. You walk out of the room into what appears to be a governmental or legislative building, then down some steps into a large foyer. It reminds you of state capitol buildings, and the railway station in the slow motion scene from *Untouchables*.

You could be in danger from those guys. You decide to get the hell out of there calmly but quickly.

4/14

For a long time, you travel many roads with a map that assigns names to the roads. They seem familiar, as if you know them from Detroit or somewhere. You've been on these roads before, but it was pointless and confusing. This time, you have a definite destination.

You arrive at a long wooden one-story building like the

workhouses built for projects like the Hoover Dam. It's a deep rich brown and the surrounding landscape is white, blue, and grey. The ground has lots of limestone.

This is all in a dip, not really a valley, below the level of the nearby road. A creek runs through here at the nadir of the dip and the end of this wooden building. The building has a covered walkway all along its length, wide enough that you could put a few chairs outside the doors and still walk by. The entire structure sits on stilts, keeping it level despite the uneven landscape.

You walk all the way down to the end of this walkway, to the creek. You want to cross it but are not sure if you can do it on foot. On the other side lies a neighborhood, a suburb with better houses than where you were raised but not a millionaires' suburb. Off to your right, you perceive a bay with sailboats.

A bridge arises from nowhere. You try to activate the mechanism of the bridge to no effect. But suddenly, the platform sinks and things around you rise up, and a wooden bridge appears. It extends to the other side, stretching out from your platform.

The impossibility of it shakes you, shocks you. You look around. It is not a sunny day, slightly overcast, but it's a very cool spot here. You like this place. Maybe you should go back and get someone else.

But would that really make this place or event any better? Would they even groove on how nice it is here? Or appreciate it? Probably none of the above. Probably, they would just bring you down. You don't reach a decision so much as you stand there, taking in the beauty of the surroundings.

You wake up before crossing the bridge, but you are sure the answer is not to go back for anyone. The answer is to go across the bridge solo. If people are going to be downers, just enjoy the time you have and the journey you are on. You may not have a clear final destination, but you know you want to keep moving forward.

4/15

You're in a room, maybe your GF's place. Her cat comes in from another room, filling you with happiness. As you pet him, you realize he is cold, so cold, to the touch. Worried, you scoop him into your lap, wrap your arms around him, and pet him in hopes of warming him up. How could she let him get so cold? You're angry at her, but she doesn't seem concerned at all.

He looks into your eyes as you pet him. He loves you so much and you love him. Such a good boy. You worry about him. Why was he so cold?

4/16

You and your sister in a parking lot at night. You are Iron Fist, from Marvel Comics. Your costume is less flashy, though: black pants and a green, long-sleeve t-shirt. You are there to fight Angar the Screamer. In the books, Angar warps reality into terrifying hallucinations with his scream.

Why the parking lots? Sometimes when you and your sister were bored in Olympia, you would go to the parking lots of shopping centers, closed late at night, and sing, smoke, and play guitar where no neighbors would mind. You'd laugh and make up 'cute songs for cool kids.'

At other times in your life, you saw parking lots as a place of doom and death, populated by ravens and crows pecking at cigarette butts. A black paved plain of sadness and eternal rain. Sitting in a parking lot as a young man disappointed at the loss of his ideals and the constant tedium.

You and your sister walk through the lot and encounter Angar. You and he try to reach a decision on where to fight, but he has an accomplice. Both of them are huge, muscular, strong. He has a chin so big it hides his throat. He also holds a black billy club like the dark-skinned man. Then, a second club appears in his other hand.

The two of them challenge you to a fight. You cavalierly respond, "Sure." It occurs to you that you may get your ass kicked. You tell them to leave your sister out of it as she walks away. The accomplice trails her threateningly and suddenly punches her in the throat with his club.

You jump on him to force him to the ground. He doesn't budge. You try to get your arm around his throat, but that damn big chin blocks you. He is too much bigger than you for your weight to force him down. You bite his deltoid. In his deltoid is a little bone about the size of a fifty cent piece, but square. You get your teeth around it and clamp down as hard as you can. He swings the club at your sister again. You fear you can't win this fight.

Next thing you know, you come to as if you had been knocked out. You find yourself outside the shops at the far end of the lot, still night, and your assailants nowhere to be seen. Where is your sister?

Concerned, you start walking back to the place where the dream started. Your sister walks out of one of the stores with a box of cookies. You meet up and walk to an outdoor table where a female friend of hers sits. Your sister is fine. The two of them have been hanging out, waiting for you to come to.

You all get in a car. Her friend drives. Lanes of traffic

stretch out before you into some city. A bridge and a bay sit on the right. Then you're pulling up to a modified version of your parents' house, the driveway sloping up a small hill where the house sits.

Your parents are pulling out of the driveway, so you pull into the spot beside them. Mom's driving. She frowns at you. You get out and apologize for getting your sister into this mess. With nothing but a look of sadness, Mom tells you how disappointed she is in you. Then she backs out and drives off.

The inside of the house is like no house your parents ever owned. Sister goes all the way to the end of the second story hallway to a bathroom inside a bedroom there.

You think about what happened. You decide you can only make it better by returning to the parking lot, finding those two guys, and fighting them. You wonder why you didn't use the Iron Fist power on them. Now you fear the Iron Fist won't be enough, but your shame drives you. Somehow it's all your fault.

You walk down the hallway to a basket. You have to pee, so you pee in the basket. But there is water being pumped into the basket, so it starts filling rapidly. You fear it will overflow before you're done peeing.

You call out to sister that you're going to settle things with those guys.

A TV show introduction interrupts the dream. It's a cross between *Hill St. Blues* and *Cheers*, with a theme song, and the main characters wear too much black like priests at a funeral. The camera focuses on an old woman.

Now you're in a room. You've joined the priesthood as an initiate. You and the others get ready, get in line for the induction ceremony. Everyone wears gray uniforms with hats like Canadian Mounties hats. Perhaps they are drill instructor hats. This is the warrior/priesthood.

The guy behind you makes a pass at you. He wants to touch your ass and fondle you. You decline, wanting nothing of the sort.

You walk over to the bed. Your black pants are there from the beginning of the dream. They lay front-down. On the ass of the pants are two pieces of paper. You pick them up and study them. There's an address telling you where the guys from the beginning of the dream are now. It's almost as if you've gone undercover in this scene to uncover their whereabouts.

As you study the pieces of paper, you realize you are back at the house from earlier, still studying them. Now one of the papers has become a pamphlet, a brochure, with an address on the back. It's hard to tell what the address is. The brochure has a picture of a tower or building with a third-story patio/balcony that grants access to the building. Chairs sit on the patio. This seems to be where you will find your assailants, or at least some key to the resolution you seek.

You can do more than use the Iron Fist as a club, so much more. You can also heal. The manual is in the golden, glowing book of all Iron Fist knowledge. You need to integrate your power with a transformative solution, or you will battle these assailants forever, in different forms.

Again you announce to sister that you're leaving.

4/16

Chris and about two dozen other people give a singing performance from a raised platform in an atrium filled with plants and a man-made stream flowing through it. You recline on a bench to enjoy it, apparently the only person in the audience. Chris talks to someone who works there about how no one showed up, jokingly referring to "all these people" as if embarrassed by the low turnout. But it's a very pleasant afternoon not unlike the vibe today at the Nursery where there was art in the garden.

You're in a gift shop/café talking to a woman about music performances at the venue. You look at cards, maybe some food. She points out something on a bookshelf.

As you look at it, it becomes an old comic book, modeled after old DC horror comics or the EC line. It's entitled *The Fate of Fear*. The bookshelf slowly becomes a shelf of comic books, changing shape. The room changes shape around it, too, becoming more like a comic shop.

You wake up in the upper bunk bed you had as a kid in the room on Highview. Mildly annoying 1980s pop music plays. You get up and climb down from the bunk bed in the dark. As you reach the floor and walk towards the door, you see the pop music comes from a radio your sister is cuddled up with in the lower bunk. She's sound asleep. You consider turning it down or off but don't. How can she sleep with that crap playing? She must find it soothing.

You exit through the door and the layout is exactly like Highview: doors on the right to your parents' room and Dad's study. Inside the bathroom, though, it's really big, not the small Highview bathroom. It has a row of urinals, all tiled surfaces, two sinks, like something you'd expect at a hotel.

You're naked except for your socks. You pee and wash your hands. Your friend walks in. He's also naked and only wearing white socks. You greet him and he says, "Hi." You exit and walk down the hallway to where the living room would be, but instead it's a comic book shop. You make a loop, wandering through the stacks, looking at cool comics until you come to a long countertop.

The guy who will ring you up uses a magnetic stick to pick up a small metal flask-shaped pipe. It's smaller than a Zippo. He asks, "Would you like one of these, sir?"

You say, "Yes! I would!" He demonstrates how it opens, where the pipe is stored, and the poker to clear the pipe if it gets clogged. Neat little device. You think about how you would never get it by a metal detector, but it looks fun to take places in your pocket.

4/18

Night. You and your sister take a car to a house where some kind of party is happening. She drives.

Led Zeppelin rehearses in a room upstairs. The party room is expansive, dark, and covered with lots of wood. A single pile of rubbish, and the rest of it is empty.

You sing as if you're part of the band. It feels good. Uplifting. You go outside and look at the lawn, then you're back in the car with sister.

A woman crosses the crosswalk in front of you. Sister looks the other way, checking oncoming traffic to the left as she turns right. She misses the woman by inches. It concerns you that she didn't see the woman and almost hit her. You don't want to be critical but maybe you should say something to her.

4/19

You confront a figure. You try to stab it with something sharp before it touches you with its creepy skeletal hand. It looks like a cross between Jim Starlin's Death and an evil Jawa, two eyes shining inside its head, like electricity.

Later on, you move out of one apartment, time passes, and you get ready to move back in. As you move out, your roommate leaves you a book taped to the wall and says to look inside.

You take it from the wall. It's all taped up in clear packing tape you have to rip open or something. He's left you some cash inside the book, but not as much as you expected. A five, some ones, a ten.

In the book you see different articles and headlines. One is a study of dogs or wolves, pictures of a naked guy with little brown wolf cubs in one of those fake zoo enclosures for animals. What is he doing standing there? It must be some kind of study, or maybe he's training them or displaying dominance or something.

You take a walk through the city until you're in your new place. You talk on the phone to some guy who tells you your old apartment will be open. He mentions that your landlord will have it available soon. He calculates your rent and says that over the next three years your total payments will be $400,000. But, not to worry. It only comes out to $415 per month. Apparently your dreaming brain does not do math very well.

Then a bunch of guys come over, some old friends and acquaintances. You all order pizza, chips, and dip. You just hang out, eating, kind of celebrating your move out. You tell somebody to get some more to drink because you're out.

4/22

You're driving. Someone's in the passenger seat. Sister's in back. She's embarrassed about something in the glove box. You drive the Grand Am on a path through a forest. Fallen trees bar the way, but you plow through them. You revel in your own active, decisive power. Some of the trees can't be plowed through, so you get out and move them.

You walk down paths with some guys including a childhood friend. He falls in a hole or a big depression. You give him advice on getting out, and he does. He goes and climbs on something, a column on a building that's before you.

You enter the building. You like this place. It's modern and well-lit with lots of windows and surrounded by forest that reminds you of Rockwood Reservation.

On the second or third story, a bunch of people gather, mostly females, sitting four to a table. It's a large, long dining room full of windows, entire walls of windows looking into the forest. You are all celebrating something, maybe your birthday. This isn't where you planned to celebrate, but it's a good spot.

You sit at a four-top and the girl to your right is the helpful chick from class. The girl across the table is the pretty girl from another class. She leans in to talk to you, and you lean in to listen. The two of you are cheek-to-cheek, and the feel of her face against your right ear is exquisite. Calming, peaceful yet stimulating. The exquisite pleasure of contact, connection, mingled with desire.

4/28

More than twenty-four hours pass in one of your long travel dreams. You travel through forests, take a car on some roads.

A thin blonde woman in her thirties and a little girl appear. The little girl is quiet, serious, maybe slightly sad about something but not fussing about it. Your focus is on the little girl. You take her to a cabin or a shack. It's rundown but sturdy. It's open on one side but reasonably comfortable: warm, dry, sheltered from the weather. It's a temporary place for her to spend the night in safety.

You have to go but plan to return. You have a GF at home you need to see, and you're concerned she will be suspicious about this travelling. You leave for the city, or home, after conversing with the blonde woman about the girl's safety. A ghostly flicker of her face as she turns away. Your own face shows stubble, and in your gray parka you look like you've been roughing it for a bit.

When you arrive at your destination, the young girl is there but she has grown up considerably, aged in years not hours. You get confused about how she can be here but eventually accept the reality of the situation. You hug her and talk with her. As you talk, she continues maturing, and the two of you become physically closer, more intimate but not sexual.

The feeling of desire begins and causes you concern. It makes you uncomfortable that just the night before, she was a little girl! You had established another kind of bond with her, not a sexual but an emotional bond.

Your brain struggles to resolve the reality of her visible aging process here. Soon she will appear to be in her twenties. Which female is which? You worry about being discovered by your GF, but... isn't she the person you came to see, who is now this girl? What is going on?

4/29

You walk into a clothing store in a mall through a ground-level entrance. A series of walkways, gardens, and courtyards fill the building. Looking around, you see lots of clothing, mirrors, women shopping, a girl at the counter. You are underdressed in black t-shirt, shorts, gloves, and some old Chuck Taylors. Sunglasses. The kind of shit you wear all summer.

You try on a gray suit coat and black pants. A black tie and a white shirt. The coat is soft, something substantial like wool but soft like flannel. You really dig the coat. The girls remark how nice you look. You model in front of the mirror for a few minutes like it's a photo shoot. The suit looks more like Huey Lewis material than CEO style. But you really dig the look and feel. It's the first suit you ever felt at home in, and you're excited to wear it.

5/09

An outdoor gathering includes some of your past jam buddies. A procession of friends, objects, and people curves through the air above a huge water-filled hole in the ground. A berm surrounds the hole, giving it the look of a crater. You all hang out inside in it in the water.

Later, you find yourself in the back of an old Chevy pickup truck. Your friend comes in through the rear passenger door across from you. Since he's not driving, the truck goes out of control.

He scrambles out the door trying to climb around and get back in the front. It doesn't go well. The truck barrels towards a block wall fronted by little bushes. He gets back in but can't get to the brakes in time. You reach for the parking brake, pulling it, straining. He also grabs it and applies pressure. The truck stops inches from the wall.

That evening, you and he talk on a porch. You move some things out of the truck and then have tea in little teacups. You tell him how you had sex with two chicks that day, one before the party and then one at the party or shortly afterwards. You tell him this earnestly, as if it is your reason to live.

5/12

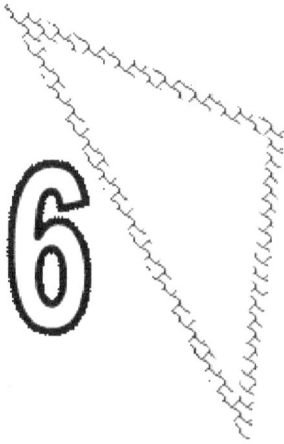

You are trying to solve a visual problem of getting a number and a shape to fit together. The number is six. The shape is an obtuse pink triangle, black or empty on the inside but delineated by an outer pink line that's fuzzy or bumpy, a kind of ripple.

5/13

Landscapes. Train tracks on a white gravel bed through a pine forest in full green. Midwestern lakes from an aerial view.

Then, an overlay of a screen: a Facebook feed. You converse with some high school friends about an offer one has to each pay $500 for tickets to a nature trip, then resell the tickets and make money. You worry it means you won't be able to go on the trip, but you say okay. Minutes later, the FB feed shows your credit card has been charged.

Now you stress out because you don't know which card or if the balance will leave you enough to live on. To add to the confusion, you believe the charged card only has a $100 maximum charge limit. The card is like a hotel key, with an arrow on it, and a smiling bear, like the Sugar Crisp Bear. Will you be able to use the funds if the charge is declined?

The scene shifts back to more aerial views of nature and forests, train tracks.

You're in a small room, a cell, or somewhere revolutionaries gather. It contains a bed that's more like a bench and a single light bulb with a lampshade hanging from the ceiling casting a circular spotlight in the middle of the room. Some light comes from the doorway. A man by the door leans back in a chair. He wears a beret and a rifle. The nature trip tickets are still under discussion, and your high school friend, the one who had the idea about the tickets, appears in the room with you.

5/20

You find yourself in a large, spacious sci-fi/fantasy building. Then, you're looking at John Cassaday's drawings for the place. First you see the colored pages and then some finished inks without color. You admire the depth Laura Martin's colors bring to his art. In the drawings, the inhabitants of the building wear armored suits similar to *The Predator*.

You look at a drawing of a room. It's sideways, sepia toned with ink wash effects, and filled with strange humanoids. When you turn the drawing sideways, you find yourself inside the room. The humanoids are naked with big bellies and awful skin like burn scars or leprosy. They frighten you but seem to be milling about on their own, unconcerned with you. The walls resemble a cave's interior. The humanoids move as a group to the far side of the room and shuffle out into a hallway.

You go the opposite way into a bathroom with a tub/shower. Your GF sits in the tub, fully clothed. The two of you discuss the humanoids for a minute. Then some chunky girl in a red skirt and bikini top walks in. There's something over your face, like a book you're holding, preventing you from seeing her all at once. You see her exposed midriff and sides, fat roll, boobs in the red top. Then she leaves.

Your GF asks you, "Is she a 'G'?"

You don't know what that means and ask, "A 'G'? You mean like, 'Whassup, G Money'?"

Next, you dream about going to an urban sidewalk café. You sit at a table with a woman but don't talk to her. She seems to be with somebody, but you just need a place to sit. Your friend appears at another table, and you mouth the word, "Hi."

He looks but doesn't respond. Then his former GF sits with him, soon joined by an old high school friend. You go over to their table, and your friend says, "Oh, is that your thing? You don't know them, so you don't talk to them?" It isn't the welcome you expected, but then you all order food and drinks.

Soon you realize you are dreaming. You try to bring this up three times to your friends, but several things interrupt repeatedly: the waiter visits the table, you order food, people are conversing. You try to hold on to your lucid awareness but lose it.

Next you dream you have a computer and monitor in your bed and some porno mags. You're trying to look at porn on your computer, but your family is outside the room in your apartment. You try to get situated but have zero privacy. The door won't stay shut, and Dad pokes his head in. You wedge your tall chair against the door to keep it shut so you can look at porn undisturbed.

Next you dream you're in one of your childhood bedrooms. Dad's room is next door. Chris is there and you experience a sensory mash-up of them both being in the room and also being by a campfire in the woods listening to the fire. Chris has one bed, and you have another and the two of you are shooting the shit about something. It's fun being with Chris, talking. Listening to the campfire, although you're in a bedroom where there is no fire.

5/26

Bowling in a bowling alley with your sister and some old friends. Some girl comes up and starts hanging on you, her arms around your neck and shoulders. You say, "Your name isn't ... —is it? Because there was a girl here named that and she was really annoying me."

She says that isn't her name, but the comment puts her off and she walks away. You realize you implied she was annoying, and then consider that it was the truth. You didn't like the way she was clinging to you. She was pretty cute, and that was the only reason you endured her at all.

Then you go back to bowling, but you are being inappropriately loud and you know it, as if you're trying to compensate or cover up what just happened. You have a bright orange and pink bowling ball made from a soft rubber/plastic material.

Instead of bowling in the actual lane, you're about to bowl into a corner behind a vending machine which, around the corner, has a tiny hallway and a door. Before you can bowl, the Incredible Hulk appears in that spot with a brown-haired girl. Maybe it's his pal Betty.

They're in the way of what now appears to be a set of pins where the doorway was. You wind up to bowl, but they're in the way and you have a very narrow path for the ball to travel. You start trying different angles to see if you can manage a direct line from here, past the wall, and through that door around the corner.

Next, you're at a house party with a crowd of punks and alterna-teens from high school in a basement waiting for a band to play. You're on guitar in the band. There's a drummer, maybe a bassist, and Eric on vocals. You're stoked to jam, but nobody knows any songs or has any idea what to do.

So, you all aimlessly try to get your shit together and the full basement gradually clears out. That's the end of your set. You missed your chance. They'll have another band on soon.

You go out to the porch and have a drink. It's after sundown and more people are showing up.

Next you end up in some bar that's painted all black watching Bill play on stage. Some guy chats with you about guitar because you brought yours. You realize you have all your pedals and gear at your feet, so you start showing him your different effects settings. You don't become lucid, but it does cross your mind how strange it is that all the pedals are there.

You feel bad because now you aren't paying attention to Bill, but you figure he won't be too hurt since he's a guitarist too and knows what it's like. Then Bill comes over and sits down with you and starts talking guitar with you. You play a little lick he told you to practice, a banjo roll, with the fingering he showed you. This is a roll he showed you in real life and you are playing it perfectly in the dream.

5/28

You dream you and your GF and her cat are all in bed, and you receive a package wrapped in a fuzzy blanket. You open it. It's another cat, black, male, with a low bass meow.

5/30

You go to a bar in a college town you've visited before in your dreams. A band plays in a little while. You sit at a tall bar table. Some chick and her friend come and sit with you. You aren't very interested in them, but you might entertain their advances if they initiate. You all don't talk much but end up being seated at a much larger table that seats eight.

The waitress comes to take drink orders. You discuss the price of pitchers. The girls want the same brand of beer you do. Are we ordering two pitchers, or will we share one? Are you just sharing the table or are you sharing drinks and the tab?

The waitress is an administrator at the college. She wears a t-shirt and one of those half-aprons cocktail waitresses wear. The table fills up with other people, and you try to get an order for pizza together.

The large menu in front of you has a picture of the pizza: a big rectangle divided into eight lettered pieces:

A	B	C	D
E	F	G	H

The waitress says, "Matthew gets the piece labeled H." You like that, since that's your initial. But you wonder if you will need more than one slice, which means you'd need to place your own order. Are you sharing with the group or on your own?

Next, you examine documents on a table in a nearby classroom. There's something for you: a letter on blue paper in an envelope. It looks like it was done on a typewriter. The typed signature reads as the name of your waitress!

A guy walks into the room. He reminds you of your friend and someone you met before. You talk about something and notice the way he talks is weird. His lip makes a little snarl when he talks. He walks around the desk, along the wall with the chalkboard, to the door.

6/3

A large room with a stage. The room is rectangular, two or three stories tall, with a door to the outside at the back corner of the stage. You set up your guitar gear on stage, waiting for the rest of the band to show up. Your band is the opening act. The headliners have their gear on stage but the huge stage leaves lots of room for you.

You chat with some high school friends. You notice bleachers along the walls, like a high school gymnasium, the kind of bleachers that pull out or unfold from the wall.

After a while, it doesn't seem like anyone else in the

band is showing up. Just you. You tear down your gear. You lost your chance to play. You talk to someone about the headliners coming on next. Disappointing. What the fuck was that all about?

Later you're in a school which seems to be an architectural extension of the stage/gymnasium but reminds you of University of Michigan buildings. Some of the school friends from earlier are here.

You are followed into the men's room by another guy. He gets you in a hold and tries to force you to the ground. He intends to rape you. You resist. You fight him off. You escape through the door.

You tell some people the guy tried to rape you. Some seem sympathetic, and some don't believe you and try to brush you off. You are sure he's on the loose and will come after you again.

You go outside, and it's night. You see a gray cat on the sidewalk and know that the guy who tried to rape you has changed into this gray cat. You begin struggling with the cat. You know if he has a chance to change back into human form he will attack you again. You strangle the cat as hard as you can. You don't want to give him a chance to breathe, or he might change back.

You feel very bad about killing this cat but remind yourself you can show no mercy. It isn't really the cute kitty. It's the rapist in disguise. You redouble your efforts. The cat fights back fiercely, but you keep crushing its throat with your bare hands as hard as you can.

You squeeze so hard that you crush the throat completely and sever the head from the body. The body falls to the ground leaving you holding the dead bloody cat head in your hands. Mixed with the sadness of killing the cat, you feel a grim triumph and stoic satisfaction that you have eliminated the problem for good and will never be attacked by that creep again.

6/4

You walk into a restaurant kitchen that feels familiar. You look for something on the rack of pots and pans. There's an office door to the right, a metal structure to the left, either a pick-up for food or a drop off for dishes. There's a grill on the other side, burners and vents. A little hallway between that and the pot rack.

Then you have a conversation with someone about the thing you're looking for, but they aren't there. Just a voiceover. As you move around the pot rack, everything is different. Where the chef's office was now appears a DJ booth. Below the window sits shelving full of records. You look through them for a while.

It's like heaven. Peaceful and absorbing. Along the wall, the passageway that used to wrap around the grill is now bookshelves. The grill is now a metal row of library shelves full of reference books. It even has little reference cards like the card catalog. Some are overflowing with cards, and they are all covered with fascinating information. It's like being back at the artist's.

An old friend from the station stands over your shoulder rapping with you about a book on the shelf. You pull out the book and it's awesome! Small, but thick, and full of amazing, detailed illustrations in a classic style. Further in, you find interesting experimental text effects. Diamonds of white space making shapes in the text. Showers of periods dripping through the text onto a panoramic drawing in the bottom margin. Your friend narrates some of this for you. He has read it before and gives you the background and commentary.

6/10

You get on an airplane and fly to another city. It's afternoon when you arrive. You survey the landscape and the city and the buildings.

You stand by a large glass and steel building. It reflects the sky in a crystal clear blue. The sun sets and soon it is dark. You meet a girl from high school. She invites you up to her room. This building looks like an office but must be a hotel with rooms.

You look forward to changing clothes after the flight and relaxing. But you get the vibe that she wants you to stay there with her, in her bed. The possibility of sex is exciting, but isn't she married? Oh well, whatever. Roll with it.

But it doesn't happen. The two of you end up going back outside to get some food at a little restaurant across the courtyard. Some other people from high school are there. You walk around the outside of the building, looking in the windows. It's a little one-room affair that looks like a generic food shop in a shopping center plaza. Nothing fancy. Fried chicken or tacos or something.

Later, you all go to a house where the loosely scheduled "night before the reunion party" party will be held. Not many people arrive. You and the girl are in a bedroom and again the possibility of sex comes up but fails to materialize.

The two of you go outside to a large, open backyard and hang out in a sitting room with a few guys. It's daylight out now. Dennis and Cindy are there. A girl comes in and it takes a minute for you to piece together that it's Shay. You address her by name, and she says, yes, it's her.

You go to the kitchen to see what's in the fridge. You look for some beer for you and Chris. Later you find a beer from another fridge. They have two kitchens here. You're disappointed that not everyone you wanted to see has shown up yet.

Adam was in the backyard and you two decide to go for a walk together. You walk through a nice city: clean, spacious, lots of green grass. On your right appears a really interesting building. The first story is concrete, with a second story composed entirely of reflective glass windows. A blue stream runs by the building.

You stop to check it out. Adam says it has something to do with his mother, so you both walk around it. You stand in the shadows of trees off the back of the building. Looking up into the clouds, you see a progression of giant white birds flying overhead in the clouds. You point them out to Adam and say how awesome they are even though they are CGI. They have an unreal, animated aspect to them, almost ghostly, but beautiful. You both really enjoy them. They clarify into giant white pterosaurs with pointy crests on the back of their heads.

The two of you walk to the stream and discuss acting in a philosophical context for a minute. You mention that it's hard to tell sometimes if you are really being yourself or just acting out a role. He says he knows the feeling. You ask, "Isn't it hard when you're an actor to know when you are not acting and just being who you really are?" He has a look of deep recognition on his face. "Oh yes," he says, "it is."

You continue to explore the stream together. You lay on the ground on your stomach looking into the water, enjoying the grass and the sun and the sound of the water, looking at plant life and looking for any interesting animals.

Later, everyone meets in a classroom with a chalkboard. More people have joined the group. They seem like amalgams of real people, their faces, clothes, and names all combinations of people you know. One of them you recognize but can't recall the name, so he's writing his name on the chalkboard.

6/11

You are a child sitting on the floor looking at photographs with your mother. This place feels like home, but it's no house you ever inhabited. Mom wants you to pick out some photos for an event. Easter or something. She's collecting them in a special book for a craft.

You flip through the pictures. Wow! Did Mom take all these? There are family shots, some of the family on horseback, some incredible landscapes with an aerial view, black borders framing the photos. You pick out a few that you like and think will also make Mom happy.

Then you walk to a bookshelf. Most of these books belong in another section of the shelves. One is by Mark Twain. Some are about your family. One is a book of everything you need to know about what happened in the last five years: a historical almanac.

You wonder about Mom's memory. Does she have these books because she's starting to forget things? One of these books looks interesting. You want to read it later.

6/13

You were in an administrative building on a hill above an

open amphitheater-style courtyard. The amphitheater is a meeting place made of stone and concrete, a pale yellow color, circular in design, with chairs and tables made from stone blocks.

In the building, you met with the guys. One was being snippy and irritating, so you shouted him down, yelling that all these problems were the result of his being a complete dick. He shut up and you left. You walked outside past the round meeting place and around the other side so as not to be seen by anyone. You'd been in a preliminary meeting and the official meeting was to be held soon in the round place. But you had enough of dealing with them and decided to bail. Fuck it.

You walked down a giant set of steps to a road below, then to the junkyard. The junkyard sat at the back of your house.

In the junkyard, you have a cat in a cage in a broken down car. You adjust the interior to make the cat comfier. Suddenly it's two cats. One goes inside a little box you put on its side for the cat to sleep in, and one crawls up on a pillow you put beside the cage. They seem very happy and cuddly and comfortable. It makes you smile. You pet them lovingly.

6/15

Walking to the elevators with weird doors that remind you of toilet stalls. Two guys arrive on your floor. You see the display inside the elevator. It's what they were looking for, some video game system.

You take them back to an area that has what they need, but all the staff are lounging around and fucking off. You worry at first but say fuck it. You leave them all there.

You walk to some fucking house. You have no idea what this place is, do you? Looks white trash. Two white trash chicks live there. Ugly fucking furniture. A dull, overcast day.

Then you're going out with your GF. You both get dressed up in a rockabilly style to go to a music club or for some dancing. This part is fun, hanging out with her.

Then you're in an urban lot in the afternoon, seeing your shoes, dancing again. You sit on a ledge with her at the overpass where the bridge goes over the 51 highway. Some guy comes up and, after a friendly chat, he inquires about your habit of riding your bike and smoking. He asks if you're trying to kill yourself.

You say, "Yeah, but how much money will I make?"

GF says, "Yeah, that's it exactly!"

7/19

You're looking for comic books and dinosaur books in a bookstore. It has tons of shelves, both library style and bookstore style. You have an armful of maybe four books. Then you discover a giant Godzilla book. It must be three feet wide and three feet tall.

You open it up. The pictures are awesome, from every Godzilla movie ever made and every Godzilla appearance ever. It's a giant-size Godzilla blow-out! It's bigger than any book you've ever owned. Since it's so big and you want to shop a bit more, you leave it on a table.

Then confusion sets in. You look around for where you set your other books. Your browsing takes on a frantic tone. Then you see a guy reading the Godzilla book. Fuck! You go up to him and say, nicely, that you really want to buy that book. He gives a noncommittal response, like maybe you'll get to buy it and maybe you won't.

How far are you willing to take it? What if he tries to buy it? How forceful should you be? You want to buy it badly enough that you're willing to fight him for it. But he eventually just walks off. You buy all the books and go out to your car.

On the way to your car, you encounter two people who seem to be the parents of the girl in your neighborhood when you were a kid. They look like grandparents now and it occurs to you how long it's been since you were a kid.

As you get ready to drive away, the point of view shifts. You see from an aerial view outside the car. You see the store and parking lot on the side of a huge rock, a mountain. Fuck! Where are your books?

You stop and look around inside the car. Did you leave them in the store? Is your Godzilla book missing in action? Will someone else get it? No. They are on the floor in the back seat. You move them up front.

The location cuts to a shopping center in your neighborhood. Your sister is with you, and she's driving. You arrive at a home you share and awkwardly bump into each other putting your stuff down. You talk and then go outside because you left some of your books in the car.

7/28

You're assembling a blog post about the Black Panther from images and text. Then you answer questions about the economics of his reality, such as how the expenses of T'Challa's superhero activities and technology affect the Wakandan economy.

8/08

You were talking to the hot girl from high school in some outdoor café in a city from a Renaissance painting.

8/15

Lots of people gather in a mansion/resort with a sandy area out back. Greg was there and you had a feeling of great happiness seeing and talking to him. Jay, Patricia, lots of people there. You talk with many of them.

8/15

You meet a girl named Jill Reinhold. You don't know any Jill Reinhold. In her apartment, you see her bare breasts, and suddenly you are all about this chick. You see her fully naked. There is something a bit square or boxy about her body, but her skin is radiant. She may not be a ten but this glowing quality... It overwhelms you, her beauty, you want her.

You try to get your act together to maneuver the situation into sex. She gets up to go to the kitchen and make some food, but on the way she turns on the TV. You hate TV and are instantly turned off.

8/17

The dream begins as a violent mass of chaos, bodies. You fight them off for survival. They all have an infection that makes them crazed: driven to rape, torture, mutilate, dismember. You could become infected from them.

Next, your friend is with you. You've both escaped the

mob and gone into a subterranean passage, a giant tunnel strewn with rocks. A creek runs through it.

Figures shamble around in the darkness. Are they infected or not? It's hard to tell, but you decide to be cautious. At one point, the two of you try a pathway up the side of the tunnel but are confronted, boxed in, by some creeps. The may not be infected, but they threaten you anyway.

Soon, you both emerge into a safe haven of un-infected people. They're having a party on a large system of wooden decks that connect all the dwellings and serve as a communal space. It seems built into a surrounding network of shopping centers and apartments.

A woman plays a piano and sings jazz songs. She has chocolate brown skin and curly black hair. Indoors, she wants to have sex with you. You worry because she exhibits signs of infection. This village is supposed to be free of infection. Should you tell someone? You want her but worry you'll get infected through saliva or sexual fluids.

She says you can't get infected that way. But, she would say that, wouldn't she? She wants to do it in the shower. She starts up the water and gets in. Your stomach aches and there's only one place to shit: in the bathroom by the shower. She is grossed out and leaves the room. But when you get in the shower, she comes back in and gets in with you.

Later you dream of another tub in another bathroom. Your friend is there with you, dressed in black. In the tub is a female body you can only see from the navel down. He uses his fingers to demonstrate a method of stimulating female sex organs.

Later, you come home to a rectangular multi-story brick apartment building adorned with columns. Metal stairways wrap around the building. You have some old comic books you are excited to check out.

In the parking lot, this bald guy swipes them from you, but you catch him. You brutally pound his face into the brick walls and pavement. He seems to have stashed the books somewhere and also ripped off one of the covers. It lies on the ground. He doesn't want to tell you or give you back the books.

You shout, "WHERE ARE THEY," smashing his face into the bricks repeatedly. The bricks shatter. That mother fucker. You keep smashing.

8/23

You and Chris go camping together. You start your journey in a vast underground concrete tunnel or passage. Eventually you come to a concrete wall with a narrow opening, a break in the rock rather than a carved opening. He makes it through to the other side. You follow. It's very narrow, and you really have to squeeze to get through.

The two of you camp for days in the forest. One day, while walking around, you encounter a small western town that seems right out of *Little House on the Prairie*. Even Michael Landon is there.

But the house is being sucked into a giant hole in the ground, a kind of violent sinkhole that draws in all the buildings and people, and even your tent! It occurs to you that the tent sucked anyway. Your phone almost goes in the hole, but you rescue it. As the town sinks, you comment to Chris that the town was too stupid to live anyway.

The two of you walk back as you review all the stuff you lost. Finally you come back to the crack in the wall. This time, instead of squeezing through, you wedge yourself in and push. It reminds you of Samson and the pillars. You worry the whole tunnel might collapse like in the Samson story, but you succeed in widening the hole with will power and muscle power. Now it's big enough for you to walk through comfortably!

Further along the tunnel you find a book fair. Chris wants to stay and help set up. You're only interested to see if they have comic books, which they don't. When you mention comic books to one of the organizers, he says, "They're called graphic novels now."

From a large chest you bring out a copy of a big book of "Action" games with Superman on the cover. That's the only thing remotely comic book they have. You and Chris leave, heading towards a large exit to a brightly lit city full of cafés.

8/24

A sedan arrives to pick up you and Dad. From the backseat, you recognize the driver. He takes you to a shopping center.

Cops pull up behind you. The driver is not pleased, and the cops just sit there while he pretends to not notice them. He backs into their car with a loud smash!

The collision derails an invasion of the shopping center by about eight cops. The raid involves some kind of child labor or child slavery. Interrupted by the crash, they come over to help their cop buddies and are all angry with the driver. You get a sense he purposefully wanted to interrupt this raid. Is he in on the child labor racket?

Next, you are all in handcuffs on your knees on the pavement in a circle with people from the store. The cops question you.

8/24

You paint a small box made of handmade paper. You paint the outside yellow and the inside black. Your friend is there, in a warehouse or auto shop, or combination of the two. You paint random symbols on a glass pane framed by wood. It's like a window, only smaller. You just keep adding more and more to it, having fun with it. It looks kind of cool, and your friend comes over to check it out.

But playing in the background is a horror movie. As the movie gets more graphic and involved, it takes over the dream until you are inside it. A girl gets chased through a creepy house by some undefined horrible thing. She ascends the stairs all the way to where they end in an attic. In the attic, a dead girl hangs from the rafters, seemingly tortured to death. The ceiling is red and bloody. The horrible thing appears and threatens the running girl. She is going to get sliced, diced, and hung from the rafters, too!

Suddenly a hole blows open in the wall. The bad guy and all the scary stuff get sucked out and blown away into the black night sky. Standing there on a small stage, like a diorama, are all the friends and family of the running girl. They ask her, "Did you really think we would all let this happen to you?"

8/25

You ride a bus with your friends and they're all acting like assholes. An old high school buddy is there, being a jerk. Your friend is there, too. But he thinks you are being the asshole, and tells you to lighten the hell up.

You walk down a country road and see people at a lake. Some of the women get in the water. You go up to a nearby house. In a room that seems to constantly shift, you find notebooks full of your own handwriting.

The room reminds you of a church or something vaguely religious. It's very formal, long, and draped in red with some gold fixtures. You explain the dream up to that point to two ladies who slowly come to realize that you are not making it up. They also realize, as do you, this must be a dream.

Some distance from the house, in a large agricultural field, you sit in a truck reading a book. Your sister comes up and talks to you for a bit. Looking at the clock in the truck, you realize it's after 4 p.m. and that your high school reunion begins at 7 p.m. But the reunion is a four-hour drive from here, and takes place in a time zone with a four-hour difference. This means it's already started, and you won't be there until 11 p.m. You jump up and get back to the house. Only now, the house has expanded to be some kind of resort on the lake.

From an upper deck, through a window, you see an old high school friend. Shouldn't he be at the reunion? You walk into a room to go see two more high school friends seated in large comfortable chairs. You're confused, because you want to go to the reunion to see them, but they're here!

So, you sit down. One of them asks if you're going to do drugs. You say, "Probably for the rest of my life." The other friends that amusing, but the first seems concerned. You say, "Look, the worst drug I do is smoking cigarettes. That's the really bad one."

He says, "Yeah."

8/25

Your fingertips get all cut up by a razor blade or something sharp, something you are handling. But it seems like it was due to someone else's negligence, and that annoys you very much.

8/26

There's a guy at the office who keeps appearing suddenly as if from nowhere. He looks like Anthony Hopkins with a head of thick, black hair that seems dyed. He keeps popping up with a weird stare on his face all the time. You tell your supervisor, who calls the guy into his office.

The supervisor asks him if he can work on a project. He describes a Martian fantasy and asks the guy to give some opinion or report. The guy gets very excited.

"Yes! Of course! That's exactly what happened to me," he says. It seems like he has finally found someone who knows all the crazy shit he's been going through, although you and the supervisor suspect the guy is delusional.

The supervisor pegged this guy's weird fantasy. You find it difficult to tell if the guy is really crazy or just acting that way. Is he overly enthusiastic or a dangerous lunatic? It's hard to tell.

8/26

You are at your high school reunion in a large theater watching a film. Everyone goes outside through a door by the screen, walking up a hillside next to a chain link fence at the end of the property. There, you talk to a girl from school. You tell her you like her writing and ask if she's having financial success with it.

You can tell from her body language and facial expressions that she is not. You tell her that a lot of people rave about having success from writing online, but mostly those are marketing people selling their consulting services. The reality is that most people are not making any money at it.

She gets upset, tearful, and frustrated. "Why," she asks, "are you bringing this up now?! Why are we talking about this here?" This makes you feel bad for saying for it, but you're not sure why she's so upset. As you try to puzzle it out, you see an office on your left and some plans on the desk. A friend appears, and you feel for a moment that maybe he is the sleazy marketing type you mentioned, with bullshit promises about lots of wealth.

The you're at the top of a landing above some stairs leading back down into the theater, but it's different now. Layers of cardboard, like giant flattened boxes, cover the stairs. A group of black men and women try to gather the cardboard and clear the stairs.

Another girl from school stands beside you. She touches you then takes her hand away. You hold hands with her and make your way down the stairs and into the lobby outside the theater. You ask her where the rest of the reunion will take place. She tells you but turns strangely silent and aloof.

You later realize you are being too shy and deferential. She gave you a sign she was sexually interested, but you failed to ask her to go somewhere else for a while, alone, or otherwise take the initiative.

You see Ross at the door. He greets you by your first name, which makes you happy. A group of you go outside towards a parking structure full of confusing stairwells.

You lead a group from the front, trying to find a path that connects to another group ascending through another section of the structure.

Around and around you go, ending up back where you started. Damn it! This goofy stair maze has you on a losing track. So, you climb over the railing and head directly towards the other group. A few people get it and follow you. You climb over the rails to join the larger ascending group.

8/26

In another theater, you watch a film about a car wreck involving you and four girls. The film includes a sequence featuring a scantily clad chick walking down a hall that seems like a science fiction set: the interior of a spaceship or some experimental compound perhaps.

It's very dark inside the hall. At the end of the hall, she comes to a thick metal door with a small glass window. She rotates ninety degrees in your field of vision and so does the hall, almost like a space station might. She pulls off her shirt and presses her tits to the glass.

Then, it isn't like you are just watching her anymore. Your face is in her tits as she manipulates her nipples. Your mouth finds a nipple and sucks at it hungrily, so enthusiastically you're afraid you'll damage the nipple. The emotions and sensations are off the charts intense. Then it passes, and you are back in the theater watching the movie. The film ends.

You and the four girls from the car wreck exit into the lobby. They are all gothed out with white makeup and black hair. They wear ripped clothing and appear covered in fake blood. They seem to be your GF and three girls from high school.

They want to re-enact the car wreck. They sit on the floor in the positions they had in the car. They shout excitedly, "Let's get in the accident! Let's get in the accident!" They're thrilled about the chance to re-enact the wreck!

8/26

You taste sugar.

9/2

It all begins with a dog you find on the beach. The dog seems pretty smart. Over time, its collar and shape change from more of a white Jack Russell like Gidget to a brownish boxer-type. You take the dog home on a leash.

The two of you go next door to someone's place, which is really just through a door on the wall. The dog sniffs something on a table. The host unleashes something threatening. The dog says, "Oh no!" Your mind reels for a second as you realize your dog can talk! The large black threatening beast seemingly emerges from a cosmic hole in the wall and takes the shape of a large black dog. Your dog wants to leave, pulling on the leash to go towards the door. Your reaction is slower.

The dog says, "Fuck! Fuck!"

Wow! It really can talk!

The bad black dog mounts your dog. You could help it escape, but just stand there holding the leash tightly. The black dog humps your dog for three to five strokes before you pull your dog away and make an escape.

Later that night, you walk through a town on the way

to your place. MX's house is on the way, so you stop in. From the bottom of the stairs, you see her poke her head out of her bedroom doorway at the top of the stairs. She looks super tired and sad. She says she's sick and not feeling well.

You go up to her room and talk for a while. She doesn't feel well. She has a new boyfriend. E-Ton or Ton-E or something like that is his name. You argue with her about it briefly but give up. Despite her sorry state, you still feel a sexual attraction to her.

Downstairs, you explain to her parents that you just dropped by on the way home. Have you made a mistake coming here? You need to leave to go get... something.

You end up looking for this thing at a multi-level bar or roadhouse. The thing is in a room on the upper level. But to get it, you have to go through all these guys who violently attack you.

At first, you try to avoid the attacks. But then, you realize this is the structure of the event. You must face these attacks and overcome them to attain the object. Furthermore, it's like getting "jumped in" by a gang, or "hazed" by a frat. If you make it, you will be "in" with them. In fact, they enjoy this conflict.

So, you cast aside your hesitation and give yourself over to taking pleasure in the battles. You fight, kick some serious ass, take some licks, but feel really, really good. You get a charge out of it! You don't have to hold back with these guys, only release your rage and will to power.

Just before you attain the object, though, the conflict abruptly ceases, and the object is removed. Everyone just wants to stand around and talk now. It's frustrating. Everyone says you don't have to fight anymore, but they won't give up the object. They usher you down this long hallway full of people. MX appears there, smiling, happy you gave up fighting.

You walk outside and the door closes, a happy moment where all seems calm. You say how nice it all was. Then you say, "Well, FUCK THAT!" You kick the door down and charge inside, taking on the guys again. You refuse to be held back from your goal.

It isn't clear what happens after that. Perhaps you visit MX's house again. But eventually you are walking through the town. It takes on a fantastic aspect, richly undulating hills with Bavarian houses, a kind of fairy tale land. A bridge crosses a wide cavern or valley, a wooden bridge made out of slats with rope railings. You must cross it to get where you are going, again towards the object which holds the key to... What? Fixing the MX situation? Easing her pain? What? Whatever it is, it becomes a kind of "holy grail" of your quest.

Suddenly, you are swarmed by dozens then hundreds of people in this fairy tale land as you cross the bridge. You try to fend them off. But it occurs to you this is your dream, in a dream country, and all these people are products of your own mind: projections from your unconscious.

So, you grab several of them roughly by the throats and shove them together. You yell out they are nothing but your own projections! You command them to merge! As you force them together, their bodies physically merge together. Two become one, and you keep shoving more of them together. You are attempting to unify them. It works, but there are so many of them that you wonder if you can merge them all together before they overpower you.

Next thing you know, you are somewhere else. You have arrived suddenly at the location of the object you seek, which you now sense is a glowing orb. The landscape reminds you of some surrealist paintings you've seen, not full of melting watches or weirdoes but an open space with an eerie calm, and expansive mood.

A one-story modernist building sits nearby, to the right. A few mysterious figures stand nearby.

On the ground before you is the object. It's a sphere with depressions on its surface, like a golf ball of Whiffle ball might have, and it is surrounded by white, angular, lacy forms, sheets of intersecting lattice material. You can't remember seeing anything like it before.

A woman with long hair stands across from you. You have a feeling for her that is like your feeling for MX, but different this time. She seems to be here to help you fulfill your quest, the final resolution of what you sought on this journey.

She explains that you have found the geographic location of the object, this energy orb, but this representation of it on the ground is only a statue. The actual orb is actually directly below us. To reach it, you must descend below the earth you stand on to the level underneath. She will help you do this by joining her energy with yours.

The two of you stand together, facing one another, your arms held out in front and resting on each other's shoulders. You willingly participate.

You can feel your energies merging to become a more powerful energy that can descend to the level below, together. Her head tilts all the way back. A powerful wind comes up and blows her hair in a strikingly beautiful way. The sky begins to glow all around you. You begin to sink below the surface of the ground together.

9/2

Later you meet a creepy dude dressed like he is homeless in a subterranean place below a huge concrete bridge, in piles of rubble and stone. He has a box of recordings. You look through them, considering a trade you might make for them. He says you will have to give him something, but that he's already had every blow job imaginable, and you'll have to do better than that.

You end up on the streets of the town from before, only it seems more like the neighborhood by the park where you played as a child. The light is strange, and you can't tell if it's day or night. You hold a long black tube to your mouth. It's about three feet long and has a black sock on the other end. You are trying to blow the sock off the end of it by sucking on the tube or something. Perhaps it is some fellatio metaphor related to the man underground. Did you get this tube in the trade?

There's a female walking her dog. Or is it her daughter? Or both? You talk to her about something briefly.

9/4

You live in a rustic house with a girl with long brown hair. You have to go somewhere, but before you leave you go to the bed where your cat is sleeping. You pet the cat.

The girl says, "Be careful of the kitten!"

You ask, "What kitten?"

She says there's a kitten on the bed by your cat.

You look under the little lump of blanket and sure enough there's a tiny grey kitten curled up in a ball. He would fit in the palm of your hand. He's so cute and sweet, all curled up. You feel a strong sense of affection for the kitten, but you need to go do this thing before you cuddle with him.

Then the girl and you are at another house. She's driving the car. You go inside and drag some guy out on the front lawn. He seems scared and pathetic. He doesn't put up a fight, just kind of freaks out. The appearance and layout of the house suggests your childhood home on Highview.

You throw the guy down on a pile of papers on the lawn. Nearby sits a little barbecue grill. The papers catch fire, but not fast enough for you. You grab a can of gasoline and dump it on the guy. Then you check your pockets for a match. You produce a book of matches, strike one, and flick it at the guy and the papers. Whoosh! Now you've got a decent fire.

The guy writhes around but doesn't really make an effort to escape. You turn away and leave him there to burn. You get back in the car. You and the girl drive away.

Your route takes you through a large city reminiscent of Chicago. It's dark and begins to rain hard. Turning to see out the window, you feel like your legs and arms and head are actually outside the door even though it's closed. This sensation puzzles you.

The two of you arrive at a building, and you go inside. It's tall, many stories with lots of stairwells. Walking around, you're aware that this is not your home, and this is not where the grey kitten is. The building becomes confusing, like a maze, like the whole city and all its buildings are now a maze you have to navigate and exit before you can get back home to the grey kitten.

9/5

It begins in a forest, a very mid-western forest with hills and little clearings and a few buildings here and there. You come upon a gathering of people. You have a friend with you.

One of you says something that angers a bunch of people. They begin to swarm around you. They're like Nazi skinheads except some of them seem like Mexican gang members. They begin an aggressive chant, pounding their fists and chanting an onomatopoeic expression, "WhackaBoom," implying they will smash you.

The two of you run but are surrounded. They close in. They grab heavy wooden picnic tables and trap you between them. Then, they begin to bring the tables together to smash you in the trap. As the tables squeeze and you feel the wood pressing against you, you begin to think about how to escape. A thought begins to form, that you may be able to think your way out of this trap.

Cut to the next scene and you're outside a building in the woods. You see a guy who looks like Robert DeNiro with a fake mustache which is starting to fall off. Soon he only has half a mustache and then none, and his facial features change so he looks less like DeNiro. At first, it seems you are watching him and another guy have a conversation on a TV. But then the point of view shifts so you are the other guy sitting across from him at a picnic table.

You go inside the apartment. The guy who lives there deals drugs, and you're there to get something else. He has a female with him. After a disagreement, the two of you begin struggling. Stuff gets knocked over, but you have him down on the floor in a mess of papers and books. Before you can beat the living crap out of him, more guys come through the door: his buddies, you guess.

They stop the fight and threaten you, but you escape through the door. Your car sits in the parking lot, but it seems more sensible to run into the woods first then back down into the lot to get your car. This takes you back into the forest where you were before.

You head towards a building which was in the background of the picnic fight scene. You go inside to a dimly lit storage room. In one wall, a pair of doors leads to a brightly lit room where an auction takes place.

Many people sit on metal folding chairs. Leaning against the door is your maple pool cue, your cue case, and the halves of your jump cue. These bastards are going to auction off your pool cue! Fuck that. You grab the cues and the case, knowing the only way out is through a patch of light in full view of everyone.

Doing your best to look like you know what you're doing and belong there, you confidently stride past these people towards an exit. Some of them see you, but you guessed correctly: they do not immediately suspect you. You exit the door free and clear. You re-enter the forest.

You no longer carry your cues and case but head to another building. The last one looked more like a lodge but this one looks like an office building. It appears empty and dimly lit. You go inside.

You head upstairs to a brightly lit office full of clutter and two people, a guy and a girl. Again, not making a scene but acting like you belong there, you head up more stairs to a second level in the office. Up there you find another cluttered, brightly lit office with parts of it under construction. It has a toilet/shower stall, as if someone could live up here for a while.

You hear voices as the people below bring someone else up the stairs. They talk about how the woman who inhabits this office is having it remodeled as private living quarters so she can work unimpeded. They open the door and walk in. You clearly don't belong here but escape without being stopped. You head downstairs and back into the forest.

You travel down some pathways and climb over the side of a parking structure that sits over a parking lot. It's about three stories up on a hillside, but there's a metal pole to climb down, almost like a kid's jungle gym.

You keep walking until you come to a large field some distance behind a schoolhouse at night. You remain stealthy, and no one knows you are here. You think of your friend Tim. If you can find him, he'll drive you back to that apartment building to recover your car. You know in what general direction it is even though you can't be sure of the exact location after all this wandering. You just know it's "that way."

Two females walk in your direction. You head into a grove of trees and large bushes to remain undetected. They walk straight towards you along the edge of the plants where you hide. You try to melt into the plants to be invisible. You can actually feel the branches behind you becoming a part of you. And you, a part of them. The females are so close you could touch them, but they don't see you. They move on, and you continue your journey.

You arrive at an airport. It reminds you of the Dallas Fort Worth airport, although it bears little structural resemblance. You think of Tim again. You need to rendezvous with him to get back to the apartments.

You meet him in the parking lot of the airport and point him in the direction of the apartments. He drives. Instead of descending into the forest, you end up in a well-to-do suburb on a high hill, a peak where you can look down and see a city below, mountains in the distance, and the surrounding forest. That's great but it's not where your car is!

You find yourself in a parking lot without Tim. You walk up to a car. Your sister is in the driver's seat and Dad's in the passenger seat. You get in back. Maybe now you can get to your car. The two of them discuss something that upsets your sister. She gets teary-eyed but starts up the car anyway and drives to where the lot meets a two-lane country highway.

You know it's a bad idea to have her at the wheel when she's crying and upset. She's going to drive anyway. You try to speak up before she gets on the road. "Can we just take a minute to calm down before we get on the road all upset and crying about something?"

But she's already pulling out onto the road as you say it, and saying it distracts her. She turns her head towards you as if to speak, her eyes full of tears... and smashes into the side of a passing car. Fuck! Now it seems like your fault for distracting her.

She pulls onto the road and then looks for a turn-off. She takes the next right, which leads down a heavily forested road to a building that looks like a repair shop and junkyard. All three of you go inside. No one's there so you look around. Junk everywhere. A little scale with numbered buttons catches your eye, as does a small white camel made of wax lying on a table.

Then two guys show up. While sister and Dad discuss the car, one guy tries to interest you in this wheel apparatus he just brought in. "Know anyone who could have a use for one of these?" he asks.

You look at it. He tells you the name of the mechanism,

some kind of nonsensical machine you don't recognize. He unscrews something in the center and shows you how when you tap on this thing, a tiny button pops out. You're not interested. "Sorry," you say, "I can't use that."

The next thing you know, the three of you are driving again. Night transitions into day. Now, two or three nights have come and gone since you started out. You decide to split off from Dad and sister. It makes dream sense but no physical sense: they are driving the car and then it's just you, still moving forward on a two-lane highway through a giant forest, but no car. They've taken a fork towards Boston.

You quickly decide to get off the main road and go over the side into the forested hills which extend in every direction. As you go over the side, you realize the trees on the hill do not grow straight up towards the sky. Instead, they grow directly out from the hillside in a line from the center.

You look around for a minute. It strikes you that in all directions you can see the tops of trees, looking like giant clumps of broccoli: rounded shapes, densely clumped together. So, while you thought you could climb down a tree to the ground, you end up climbing through upper layers of trees all the way down the hillside. You know you must be careful to test every branch and make sure it's not dead, that it's strong enough to hold your weight, and that it really is connected to a tree. One branch, clearly dead, hangs in the other branches. You test it but don't take it.

Eventually you make your way down to where you can see level ground below you. Your depth perception can't yet register how far away it really is. You climb a little more until you can tell it's about ten feet down, close enough to let yourself drop. You drop down and land just fine.

You find a crawlspace under the trees, like the crawlspaces once built underneath porches on houses. The floor is packed earth and roughly milled logs provide rectangular timbers for support. You crawl in to check it out but realize a wire mesh covers the entrance. Now you seem trapped inside it.

The crawlspace seems to extend indefinitely to the left and right. You got in but are now stuck inside. You can't force the screen open. Then a thought comes to you: Your mind can control this reality, and if you can focus then you can alter this reality so you can escape. It isn't entirely lucid. You don't realize you are dreaming, just that your thoughts can alter reality.

You close your eyes and visualize yourself turning into ooze that can pour through the mesh. You really work at this visualization until you can clearly see it happening. You feel like you're having success, but when you open your eyes you are still stuck on the same side of the screen. "Damn, that didn't work as planned," you say.

But before you can give in to frustration, you scan the length of the screen to your right again. Now, about ten feet away, a square hole appears in the screen. Just big enough to crawl through! You feel like the visualization didn't work as visualized, but your mind power created a means for you to get out anyway. You got what you needed, even if it didn't come in the form you imagined it would. Neat! You resume your journey.

You find yourself in a cross between a parking lot and a junkyard. Various cars, orderly arranged, some broken down. You're in the driver's seat of a truck. It has a wooden bed and surrounded by wooden railings. You get out. Maybe Tim and Dad and sister are here, maybe not.

The dealer from earlier confronts you. He walks up to

the back of the truck with someone. He is angry and confrontational. The two of you exchange heated words about your car.

You brandish your key ring. It has a metal key with a black casing on the head, the make and model of your car stamped into it. It says Grand Am or Dodge Charger or something. It occurs to you that this is not the first appearance of the key ring on this journey, but you can't recall exactly when you saw it before. Also, you sense the make and model of your car has changed since this journey began. Perhaps it started out as a Grand Am but is now a Dodge Charger. You can't be 100% sure.

The drug dealer produces a paper flyer. It bears a black and white photograph of him, a mountain in the distance, and a rustic "old west" city street. Beside him in the photo stands B.A. Baracus from the A-Team, as if he is the dealer's bodyguard. It seems like this is a move to intimidate you.

You don't feel threatened. Instead you say, "Fuck you, where's my car? I'm going to get it now!"

Then the Mr. T figure appears beside the dealer in the flesh. You're not scared of him, and he knows it. You also sense from his lack of threatening body language that he knows you are in the right on this, and he is simply overseeing the conversation. He may be big and tough, but you don't feel you have anything to fear from him. The dealer gives you directions to the apartments from your location, and you set off to find your car.

You arrive at the apartments and locate the car. You unlock the door and get in. You happily drive off, satisfied at last.

9/7

You look at black and white comic book pages. Some of them depict dinosaurs, and some show people you know. The pages float in the air, more like tablets than thin paper pages.

9/9

You arrive at this guy's house for a party. In the foyer, you sign his guest book. He tells you that everyone at the party is having drinks with poop in them.

"Poop?" you ask.

"Yes," he says, "Every drink has a stick of poop in it."

It sounds weird, but you give the guy his guest book and enter the dining room. He is a little too fat and laughs a little too loudly. A curtain covers the wall on the far side of the dining table. In the curtain, a doorway leads to another room. Either it is a door frame with no door, or the door is open. Your GF is in that room. She sees you and starts walking toward you. Her friend sits at the table with a black, shadowy figure you assume to be her boyfriend. Her friend has a colorful bright red drink in a cocktail glass. A stick of poop like a dog turd stands straight up in her drink.

The host said we were all drinking poop drinks but the only drink you see with poop in it is hers. She laughs at it. Everyone is very chatty. The fat guy explains that they were all just sitting there when the poop fell from the top of the curtain. How did the poop get there? Is poop forming spontaneously in the curtain and falling into drinks? You watch to see if that's what's happening, but you don't see anything happening. The friend sits right under the curtain. You sit down on the side of the table opposite the curtain, next to the fat man. It's evening.

The next thing you know, you're driving a car through the streets of Ann Arbor on a sunny day. You're on your way to a party but want to stop first and get some beer. You review possible stores. You want some decent beer like Newcastle and a pack of smokes. You turn on Packard and cruise down to Sgt. Pepper's. It's been a while since you've been there, but you liked that place.

The next thing you know, you're at a large stone building. It resembles, architecturally, the Law Quad at University of Michigan. You want to get around the other side of the building to... what? An entrance?

You're up about two or three stories on a stone ledge that wraps around the building. You carefully make your way around. The ledge is wide, but every so often there's an architectural ornament or column that interrupts it, blocking your path. You must be very careful about finding handholds to navigate around these obstacles.

On the third face of the building, the ledge comes to an abrupt end at an arched and recessed window. You can go no further. However, a couple, a black man and a white woman, has followed your path and come up behind you. They wait for you to go forward so they can, too. They don't seem to understand they need to get out of your way so you can backtrack.

After some dialogue, they seem to get it but still don't make much effort to move. Somehow you get around them but continue having trouble with the architectural obstacles. You get nervous. It feels like the stone may be loose. You really do not want to fall.

Below, a huge grass lawn. People walk around. The lawn holds a temporary stage and seating. The seats, perhaps 500 of them, are covered despite being outdoors. It's pretty high-tech for what appears to be a temporary concert set-up.

Suddenly you're down on the ground near the stage. John walks by. He's dressed in all black except for a white rock band logo on his t-shirt, his long hair bouncing around. He's organizing or promoting the concert.

He turns to you and says, "The Devil Says... rrrrrrrRRRRAAAAAAAAAAAAAAAARRRHHHH!!!"

You crack up. It's a quote from the introduction to the Soundgarden song *Searching for the Ground with my Good Eye Closed*. Some dude next to you doesn't get it. You explain it to him.

"RrrrrrrRRRRAAAAAAAAAAAAAAAARRRHHHH!!!" you say, quite happily. Then, the song comes on over the amphitheater speakers. Yes!

The next thing you know, you've made it to that party. You don't recall ever getting the beer. DJ and your GF are there in the spacious, penthouse-style apartment with lots of windows. The upper level seems to be the rooftop. A canopy covers the entire space, supported by rectangular columns. A band performs on a stage. You take a seat near one of the columns, chilling out, checking out the band. They're not that great, just some classic rock cover band.

The band mentions something bad that just happened. A voice from behind you says, "You did it, didn't you? Didn't you? You're the one who did it!" You turn around. It's your GF's friend accusing you of doing this bad thing. She's in your face repeatedly accusing you in a mean, nasty way. She won't cut it out. You grab her by the hair and pull her out of the seat. You slam her face into one of the columns once, twice, three times. It looks like it hurts. You don't really feel bad about it. You just want her to shut the fuck up. The accusations make you angry. You throw her roughly to the floor.

You ditch the scene and go downstairs, all the way down to ground level and exit to a large wooden porch, a covered deck that wraps around the building. Two or three steps lead down the yard.

As you're about to walk down and leave, you see a kitten on the deck near the steps. It's not grey like before but marked more like Piper. It looks hurt, like somebody beat it up. It lies there like it's dead. You feel so bad for it.

You begin to reach down to it, then GF and her friend show up. GF feels bad for the kitten immediately. Her friend starts in with the accusations again. She thinks you hurt this cat. It quickly becomes clear she wasn't accusing you of whatever the band was talking about, but of hurting this cat.

You say, "You think I did this?! Fuck you! I did not do anything to this cat!" GF is horrified that you might have hurt the kitten, but she believes you. You reach down and touch the kitten. It moves.

It isn't dead. As it begins to move around, it becomes clear it doesn't have any injuries. You try to comprehend why it looked hurt when it isn't. Nearby sits an older cat, maybe the kitten's mother. You pet the kitten, and it seems okay. Cute little thing.

You leave it and go across the street, looking for your car. You don't see it. You can't remember at all where you parked it. You wander through vacant lots across the street. Buildings must have been here once, between apartment buildings on either side, but the lots are now surrounded by chain link fences and full of trash and stone wreckage. You think to yourself, "What am I doing in these lots? How did I get inside these fences? What the fuck am

I looking for? Oh yeah: my car. Why would I be looking for it in these lots?"

You feel confused. Directionless. Your GF's friend goes to her car which is parked on the side of the street across from the fences. She sees you as she opens her door. She flashes an accusing glance your way.

You feel somewhat ashamed that she can see you in this confused state, aimlessly wandering. You try to look like you know what you're doing but you just look clueless, and she knows it. She knows you don't have a fucking clue where your car is. You're just wandering around this stupid lot full of trash and dirt. You hope she drives away soon. You feel like you need to clear your head and get back on the road.

9/10

A guy you used to work for comes over to your house. The house is loosely modeled on a house you and GF rented once, but the backyard resembles the yard at your childhood house. The front of it, when seen from the street, appears to be a two-story affair with a porch and dark shingle siding, unlike any house you've ever lived in.

You and the guy sit next to each other reviewing some Excel spreadsheet. He works the mouse and keyboard of his laptop, and you help get the spreadsheet together. He can't get the numbers right in a certain column because he needs to clear out some formulas. But when he tries to delete them, the numbers still come out wrong. It turns out he didn't delete them all. You get frustrated because you know you can make this right in no time. "Just let me do it," you say, but he continues to fumble with it.

Now you're in a spot between the living room and

kitchen. The wall of the living room has a large sliding glass door that leads to the backyard. You stand up for a minute and notice something amiss. Although the door is partially obscured by a gaudy curtain, you can see the door is ajar. The curtain is green shimmery velvet that looks frumpy and ugly against all the beige of the living room. The sliding panel of the door has come off its track so it won't shut properly. It's open about a foot wide.

You feel a fearful knowledge the cats have all gone outside. Who knows how long they've been out? It must have been the last time GF used it, and she's been away at work for a long time. Now you're worried about the cats and angry at her.

You pull the curtain down and fix the door by placing it back on the track. It's heavy, but you get it done. You go out to the yard to look for the cats. Instead of your cats, you find two kittens and their mother. They have markings like the cat in the last dream. The kittens are big, roly-poly, dirty, having a fine time rolling around in the grass. You think to yourself, "These are the cats I have been dreaming about." You pet them for a second, but they are pretty dirty with chunks of grease in their fur.

Then [**REDACTED**]. You ask him to sell you some. He asks how much. "Look," you say, "I'll buy it all from you, or as much as you are willing to sell me."

He gets the video games set up. The sequence ends on a strange note: You're holding these little electronic gadgets you found in the kitchen by the trash can. They resemble game controllers but... they're broken or something. You look at them, fiddle with them, wonder if you can get them to work. He says they're totally fucked. You ask if you can take them home and dismantle them for a piece of artwork.

Later, you're in some kind of art museum. You're supposed to be part of a tour group there, but you fall behind them, going at your own pace. You never liked tour groups anyway: too much like a herd of sheep or cattle. The group walks down a hallway with a huge two or three-story wall of glass windows on their right. You watch them go. GF is in that group.

MX is with you. Damn, she looks good. Not really dressed up or anything. Hair in a ponytail, normal clothes. But, damn, do you like looking at her. She seems a little embarrassed when she hands you a folded roll of money. What is this?

She says, "Here's the money I borrowed from you. Thank you." But you're thinking this is the money you loaned to GF. You accept the cash but can't fully resolve this discrepancy. MX says she borrowed the money, but it's the money GF borrowed...

The next thing you know, MX is in your arms. The two of you lovingly embrace and begin to kiss. It would be a passionate moment, but your mind is concerned that you will be caught and kicked out by museum staff for making out in the gallery, or else GF will walk up and find you like this.

The emotional tone is vivid. You want to give yourself over completely to this embrace and kiss, but at the same time try to tone it down to something more appropriate. The feel of her in your arms, of her body against yours, of her lips and your lips. You rub her back, stopping yourself from rubbing her ass because, again, you don't want GF to walk up and see that. But your desire for her is so intense. The sensation of her is so overwhelming. If you could choose between waking life and just dreaming moments of this union with her forever, you'd choose the latter.

9/11

You take your scooter to the Mexican fast-food drive-through, but now it's a walk-up affair with a metal roll-away covering over the window area and a countertop. Some Mexican ladies stand in line before you, and their order takes forever. Eventually you get some food.

9/12

You converse with a small Asian female with shiny black hair in a neck-length bob and traditional garb. She leads you through passages through a series of rooms. You know these rooms are underground without really having visual cues to that effect.

You come to a room with a large wooden table. A fireplace sits to your right, recessed into a wall along with an elaborate painting looking like a window into somewhere. The female opens a door at the far end of the room which summons or releases a guy working in that room. He seems to be a king, but the room resembles an art studio.

He is unhappy to be disturbed and charges at you. The two of you flee back the way you came and lock the door behind you. He opens it anyway, so you flee to the next room, shutting the door again. These doors are all wooden, thick, heavy. The walls are all stone, a kind of stone brick, tan in color. The guy gets the door open again. The two of you flee to another room and shut the door behind you. He begins working on this door, too.

The female begins to open a door to yet another room when you think to yourself, "This is ridiculous. One, I'm not afraid of this fucking guy. Two, she's the one who let him out, so his beef is with her anyway. Let them work it out!"

You back up to the wall, out of the way, in case he comes rampaging in and storms right to the next door. The female turns to look at you, deciding to stick close instead of running.

She comes to you. As she does, she morphs from a very short human into an even smaller doll, like one of those Russian dolls-within-dolls, but with a Chinese look. She takes a position standing between your legs. The guy/artist/king comes through the door into the room, in a rage, and makes a beeline for the next door. Then he realizes you two are still in the room.

He turns to face you. He is significantly larger than you and has aspects of a werewolf: hairy, growling, claws, a wolfish face. He sees the female is with you. As he steps towards you, you feel no fear. He looks like a nightmare but doesn't feel like one. You look him in the face, calmly.

The next thing you know, you and your sister emerge from this underground complex, passing through a door that opens onto a ground-level park or playground. It reminds you of parks and playgrounds from your childhood. As you and she converse, she keeps calling you by a childhood nickname. You grab her by the shoulders and argue about your name.

She gets frustrated and angry, frowning. You wonder what is the goddamn problem? But you get a sense she will finally do what you've asked her to do. And that satisfies you.

The next thing you know, you drive your scooter through a suburb and park at a little spot by the last house on the street before a park. You hang out in the park for a while. Although it's night, a full moon renders the scene brightly. You enjoy the evening. Then a female shows up and starts talking to you. She reminds you of a girl from high school, even though it's not her.

She's cool for a minute but then gets hyped up about swinging this baseball bat she carries. She just wants to go apeshit, swinging this bat around violently.

Then your friend shows up, and some other guy. The female wants to play baseball with all of you. Just as he is amenable to indulging assholes in their little games in real life, your friend decides it's cool: We'll play. He is the pitcher, the other dude is outfield, and you are first base. The bitch almost beans you with that bat again. You just want to leave.

She pounds a ball into the outfield. Your friend comments that she sure can hit. He pitches another and she hammers it into the outfield, way past the other guy, almost hitting a couple having a date in the park on some bench. She doesn't give a damn. No apology. She seems to be in love with her own power or force and either wants to test everyone or show off without regard for consequence or injury to others.

You decide to extricate yourself from the situation. As they play, you sneak around the side of a small structure full of electrical boxes where your stuff is: your scooter helmet and your guitar case. You gather your things quickly and quietly and just go. You hope they don't see you walking because this bitch won't let you go without making a scene. Then you ask yourself how you can carry your guitar case on a scooter.

You make it to the scooter without incident. It's surrounded by cases, plastic luggage or something. Then you see part of the scooter needs to be reassembled. The whole thing becomes a huge ordeal instead of just hopping on the scooter. You know they can see you here and will know you've left.

Sure enough, here they come, bitch chick in the lead. Just then, you realize, "This is not my fucking scooter! I'm in the wrong driveway!" Isn't this where you parked before? Right up against the park?

Who knows, but your scooter is very obviously in that driveway over there, two houses down. You grab your helmet and guitar case, plus some of these other cases that were around the wrong scooter, making the whole thing totally awkward for some unknown reason. You ask yourself what the fuck you are doing. You can't carry all this on your scooter anyway, and you need to get out of here fast.

This seems to happen a lot. You have this thing you want to get done but then time seems to expand and all this complex, trivial, detailed bullshit keeps piling up, preventing you from accomplishing one small thing. Just thinking about it irritates you.

Anyway, here comes baseball bat bitch. You make it to your scooter and get ready to roll at last. She's right next to you now, yapping about some totally pointless bullshit, trying to get you roped into hanging out some more.

Just then, your GF shows up. She engages baseball bat bitch in some conversation and magically defuses the whole thing, sending her off, down the street, away. Yes! GF turns to face you, and the whole physical environment morphs around her. Before, you were outside in a driveway at a house in a suburb. But as GF turns to you, a door closes behind her, a door with a glass window through which you see baseball bat bitch walking away in the distance down the suburban street. Then, all around the door we now have walls so that you and GF are in an enclosed room.

It all seems like a natural transition. You just keep rolling right along. You're glad to be rid of baseball bitch but suddenly GF just starts babbling. Some of what she says makes sense, and some is pure babble or baby talk. She's just running at the mouth about some totally irrelevant blah blah blah blah blah.

Rudely, you say, "Did you get rid of her just so you could do the same thing and torture me with a stream of irrelevant bullshit?"

She stops, looks hurt for half a second, then says, "No." She realizes what she was doing, and you realize she was just exuberantly happy to see you. So the two of you just go on from there.

You turn to face a large closet full of clothes. You pull out a couple of things, turn around, and lay them on the bed. None of this was there before. The dream just creates it as it moves along. You begin packing clothes into a backpack, getting ready for departure. What follows leaves you with a feeling of love and contentment.

As you pack a shirt into the backpack, you take a moment to notice the shirt. It's a light sky blue with a shiny diamond pattern woven into it. That is, the weave of the fabric makes the diamonds shiny, and they alternate with matte finish diamonds. A shiny black silk tie is folded into the front. It looks awesome.

You realize this is a new shirt, not one you already own, and you ask GF if she got it for you. She says yes, she did. You thank her profusely. She admits it comes second-hand from her dad, who made a lot of money as a CPA. You say, well, even a hand-me-down from your dad is worth more than I could pay for a shirt. You acknowledge the value of the item. Then you have another shirt with the same alternating flat/shiny diamond pattern but in solid white, with another black tie. It's just gorgeous.

You worry they'll get wrinkled as you stuff them into the backpack. GF says not to worry: they may get a little wrinkled but have been treated to resist wrinkles. You think they'd look awesome even with a few wrinkles. Certainly better than your old shirts.

Then there's another shirt without a diamond pattern but with black embroidery around the collar. It's not one of the triangular folded collars but one of those single rings that buttons right around the neckline, kind of priest-like but popular with alterna-teens a few years back. The embroidery is nice, swirling shapes, artistic without being overly fancy. Perfect for you. You tell GF how much you appreciate it. It's very awesome for you.

Her mother appears and helps fold clothes. She's friendly and chatty, helping you get ready for departure. She says mom-type stuff like, "Don't forget to blah blah blah."

You think, "Man, this is so great having GF helping me out and making sure I look good, and taking care of me, making me feel special, seeing to it that my wardrobe is good." You wonder if this is what guys with really good wives feel like. Do they get this treatment? Because it's rocking your world right now.

In the final scene, you climb onto your scooter, put on your helmet and backpack full of awesome shirts, with GF at your side saying goodbye. You feel really good.

9/12

You drive your scooter on a black asphalt highway to go to work. Several times, a large truck passes you. When they do, your point of view shifts to outside and above yourself to detachedly watch yourself maneuver. Then it snaps back.

The final time is the most dramatic. The truck comes uncomfortably close. The point of view snaps to way out over your head. You look very tiny down there on the asphalt. The scooter then executes some totally impossible moves: whipping around in circles, appearing to pass though the truck, passing under a suspension bridge, doing impossible stunts. It seems to impact a couple things that would probably be fatal. Then the point of view snaps back to normal and you arrive at an office building.

You're unharmed and in good shape, but the side of your face hurts like you got hit by something. You think that you must not have been totally impervious to harm during those stunts.

Down the hall you find an office. A bunch of guys you used to work with at an IT department are there. They look a little different, but you know it's them. You realize this isn't your regular job but a temp job.

You go to the water fountain because you're thirsty, but it's a toilet. The spout is a tiny little thing wedged in where the bowl and seat meet. Water comes out in a small trickle. You basically have to smash your face up against the bottom of the toilet seat to put your lips on it to get a drink. "Guys," you say, "is this some kind of joke?"

"Ha ha ha," they laugh, "It sure is, dude! There's some water in the 'fridge there."

Ah, those guys. They're funny. You grab a carbonated beverage from a six pack in the 'fridge. It's designed to look like beer, another example of humor from these guys. It tastes okay and quenches your thirst. You step into the hall so people can see you drinking the "beer."

Then the woman in charge of the department walks

you down the hall to a well-lit atrium for your first assignment. She sits you on the floor in front of what looks like an arcade game but is playing an extended Woody Woodpecker cartoon.

A long time later, when the cartoon finishes, you go to see her again. As you talk, you get the sense that she likes you and just handed you that fun but totally bullshit assignment because she knew you'd have more fun doing that than whatever dull paperwork they do to run this place.

Later, you are on a farm. An old man has breakfast at the table. A guy or two make jokes no one finds funny. They warm up to you when you play along with the jokes. The daughter appears to be about forty but uses goofy speech patterns sometimes. She's getting married. She's outside, standing, looking at the clouds.

You go outside to see it's a really beautiful day. One of the guys points to a hillside. You can see a small herd of deer lying in a smooth depression in the hillside. Your view zooms in on them. They seem very sweet and you like looking at them. The hillside seems almost creative, revealing new things about itself as you visually scan it. A flock of sheep graze and rest in a small crevice in the hillside. You can make out a third group of animals, too.

In the final farm scene, you're sitting on the bathroom floor looking at the toilet, examining the water in the bowl, thinking how there's no lock on the door. Anyone could walk in. You wonder why farm people don't have bathroom doors that lock. Maybe they secretly enjoy walking in on people who are semi-nude and defecating or tending to personal hygiene. You consider that farm people generally enjoy sticking their noses in your business.

9/13

Johnny and Ben from the Fantastic Four confront a fiery attacker in the Baxter Building, near the entrance from the parking structure. You're Johnny Storm. While Ben holds off the attacker, you go to get Reed and Sue. Reed chews you out for being sloppy.

"There are three ways you could have got to this floor in eleven seconds or less without using your flame powers," says Reed.

Then the exact same scene replays. Ben confronts the attacker while you get some citizens out into the hall where they will be safe. Then you go downstairs to get Reed and Sue, but timing yourself. On the way back up through a shaft between floors, you brag to Reed that it only took eleven seconds this time!

Flying and flaming on is a lot of fun! On the way in from the garage with Ben the second time, you stop and wish you could have a smoke first. The males of the FF climb up this assemblage of pipes and girders way, way up in the air in the very top room of the Baxter Building. They keep a kind of boys' clubhouse up there.

Suddenly you're not Johnny Storm anymore, you're just you. You bring up the rear of the group as they discuss how Johnny felt awkward or nervous or scared. You say, "Hey, if you think you're awkward, you should have seen me talking to girls at age fourteen."

Johnny's like, "Oh yeah, why?"

You say, "Man, I was just so totally nerded out back then."

9/13

You go to Brian's, an elaborate two-story building with a chain linked fence and a highway that goes by it, sitting on a very large grassy lot. It's a nice day. Brian's brother is there, and a few of their friends. Also attending is the homeless guy that John used to hang out with and bring to the artist's. John called him Papa Skin.

You and Brian have fun talking about comic books. You eventually get super-hungry and break out some fixings for pizza. Brian has some too, so you pool your resources to whip up an incredible batch of pizzas and some smaller bagel pizzas. You have crust, he has sauce: a good collaboration.

You grab some jalapenos and spread them on your pizzas just before they will be cooked in a grand outdoor pizza oven/grill. The homeless guy brusquely says, "No Hot Peppers!"

You obligingly scoop them off the pizzas, but it really starts to annoy you. Here he is with nothing to contribute, he isn't helping at all, and he just barks this out like an order with no gratitude or politeness.

So you say, "You know, Papa, for a guy with no job, you sure like firing off your fucking mouth a lot!" That pisses him off. He stomps into the house.

The brother says, "Oh great, now he's going to come back with a knife or poison us or something."

You say, "No he won't."

You've clearly underestimated his insanity and intensity. He comes out with a long boning knife in one hand and a two liter bottle half full of clear liquid. He approaches the table where everyone is now seated, standing threateningly right behind Brian, brandishing his knife and raving like a lunatic.

In his hand with the bottle he holds a laminated sign. It has a picture of the brother and says, "THIS BOTTLE IS POISONED." It's almost like a warning to the brother not to drink it, although Papa's going to leave it in the fridge for someone else to drink.

Papa makes everyone uncomfortable and is ruining the party. The brother gets him to calm down and sit. You apologize to him, "Papa, I'm sorry I spoke to you as harshly as I did. It was totally uncalled for."

Instead of accepting the apology or offering one of his own, he just says, "Good! That's even more ironic." His face is bright red, looking downright deranged or demonic.

Whatever. You didn't want to bring things to the point of getting stabbed, but you're not afraid of this guy. You're just trying to make peace so everyone can enjoy the party like before. You turn away and let him fume. You think maybe you should fight him now, or maybe just fuck him up later. Maybe you could stab him in the skull and toss him out onto the highway. But then you realize you're happy that you made peace instead of conflict in the end.

9/15

You're in a condo that belongs to the old woman, and she's moving out. It's her last night. You feel a boyish affection for her.

9/15

You're on a family outing with your mother and sister, and you're all staying in this multi-level tree house. It isn't like a kid's tree house, but a whole house up in a tree. It's your hotel. They all turn in to get plenty of sleep before flying out the next day. What nerds.

You and GF go to a party instead at an old-west styled multi-level ranch house on a huge lot with no neighbors. You see mountains in the distance across an expansive plain. A band plays inside, and much beer is available.

You go up to this loft space overlooking a theater-style living room and the band on stage. You pick a bed and lie down to rest. You've had a lot of beer by now, and you're tired. You can see the band from the bed.

You wake up and it's the next day. Fuck! You were supposed to catch a flight! You go find GF who is going to drive you to the airport, but she's been up all night drinking heavily and is wasted. You decide to drive. You need to stop by the hotel and get your things first.

By the time you get to the tree house hotel, you've already missed your flight. Somehow, you communicate with your family. They made the flight okay but are worried. They want to come back and get you.

"Look," you tell them, "I'm entirely capable of catching the next flight on my own." But they won't listen. They have it in their heads that they need to come back. So, they do. In no time at all, they're walking up the stairs to the room in the tree-house. You're still throwing things into your backpack when they arrive.

9/15

You're at DJ's place with a few other people. His place is modern now, not like the last time. He plays a new song he's composed. He plays it through a stereo but also on a piano that has keyboard sounds. It seems full orchestrated with multiple instruments. Maybe he's playing prerecorded backing tracks and doing the singing/keys in real time.

The song is kind of a sad ballad, but really beautiful. It envelops you with exquisite listening pleasure. When it's over, you want to hear it again. You tell DJ how awesome it was. It doesn't have a lot of complex passages or changes, but still sounds amazing. So simple, yet so beautiful.

9/15

You experience multiple views from a perspective far up in the air, as if you're levitating above a forest and hills. A two-lane highway winds through the forest between the hills. A nearby building will be the airport in this scene. The bridge is in the peaks of the hills, above the road but not crossing the road, in the forest.

You walk along this wooden bridge that's part of a pathway through the forest. You enjoy the day. It's sunny, and although spots of sunlight come through the canopy, it's nice and shady in the woods. This long bridge doesn't seem to go anywhere in particular but is fun to walk on.

Eventually, you turn around and go back the way you came. A group of people appear to your left. You don't get a good feeling about them but assume they will just go about their business while you enjoy your walk. Then one of them runs up and punches you in the gut or ribs. Maybe it wasn't intended to hurt because you barely feel it. The guy says, "There! You're hit!" Or maybe, "Ha! You're wounded!"

You think, "What a freak!" You're not even hurt. Then he does it again about five times in quick succession. He runs off to his group. You wonder what that was all about. Weirdos.

When you get to the end of the bridge, the group comes up to you. The leader is a stout Asian, or maybe Samoan or South Pacific Islands. He has short spiky black hair and a white t-shirt. He threatens you, so you punch him in the face.

You bash him in the nose three or four times pretty hard. He just stands there looking mean and dumb. He knows you got the jump on him.

"Look," you tell him, "I will keep punching you in the nose and all those motherfuckers, too. I'm faster, stronger, and I will win, so why don't you just leave me the fuck alone and go about your business?"

He talks some shit.

You think to yourself, "Fine. I'm not going to stand around arguing with these morons. I can take care of myself." You turn away and continue your enjoyable walk.

Then you fly through the air, looking at the landscape below you.

The next thing you know, you're at the airport building in the same landscape. You are inside, as if you just arrived from your flight. You walk along the path for new arrivals. Near the exit, you see some commotion. Brad Pitt and some guys in commando gear carry out a paramilitary attack on the airport. Police arrive quickly.

You make it outside and watch the clash between Brad's team and a bunch of police. You clearly see the architecture of the building: reflective glass windows, concrete columns, and a drive-up entrance under a covering. It's almost a cross between an office building and a hotel.

You turn away from the conflict. It has nothing to do with you and seems to pose no threat to you.

You place your hands on a large rock that interests you.

You hear a really amazing Chris Cornell song. It's not a song that's ever been recorded. It just comes out of nowhere in this dream. More correctly, it comes from everywhere. It emanates from the landscape and you're connecting to it. Or maybe it's all in your head and you only perceive hearing it, or maybe it fills the air all around you. Either way, it's a really awesome song!

Chris sings while the bass and drums lay down a captivating rock rhythm. The guitar tones and riffs sound fresh and perfect. You think, "I should really try to remember how this goes!" It's like Chris is singing it just for you. It goes on for a few minutes, even after you take your hand off the rock and look around.

Then you fly away with it still playing in your head.

9/15

In a college classroom, the teacher asks you to help after class with something in Excel on her computer. She's looking for a file. Her screen projects on the wall and you can see her file in the file list. She couldn't find it, but it's right there.

9/16

You and GF are in the apartment from before. The building is a Southwestern stucco style. You want something sweet to drink but have no food or anything on hand. You get all set to make purple Kool Aid but... oops! No sugar.

GF says she has sugar at her apartment and why don't the two of you go over there? Plus, you can go in the swimming pool. It sounds great, and you're ready to go. But she's taking forever. And ever...

You go outside, into the street with an electric mixer like the kind used in baking. It shoots water. You stand in the street and spray water on yourself, remembering not to hold the device too close or the beaters will hurt. It's fun, and the cool water feels really good. Houses line both sides of the street. Eventually GF is ready to go, and you drive over to her place.

The next thing you know, you're telling Dad you want to go to the pool. The two of you hop in his truck, in swim trunks, with towels, and start driving to some place he says has a pool. You drive through mid-size city streets and talk about your sister on the way. The two of you arrive at a stucco apartment complex. All the yards are white gravel. White stucco walls surround the place. The buildings are shades of purple. Dad surprises you by driving up on the gravel lawn and taking the truck through the space between the back walls of the buildings and the white boundary wall.

The path curves, like the beginning of a spiral. The space between walls becomes increasingly narrow. You worry about getting stuck. Dad drives fast enough that you worry about getting wedged in. The truck can't possibly do this without getting dented and scratched. Worry, worry.

But then you relax. It's his truck, not yours, so why worry about it? If you get wedged in, you can just go out the back window and get on with your life. Dad takes the truck until it can't possibly go any further and somehow the two of you get out despite there not being any room to open the doors. Dad says, "Okay, all we have to do is climb over this wall and there's a pool."

The wall is a little high, so you stand on the back of the truck, pull yourself up, and go over. You wonder how you're going to get back over it from this side. Then you see it connects to a smaller wall you could more easily climb to get on top of the high wall. You hope Dad can handle it. He says something about it being almost perfect, as if admitting the route has a few flaws. Well, it does, but it occurs to you that this is pretty cool and adventurous for Dad to be doing and it reminds you of being a teenager.

The two of you walk across an immaculately groomed lawn in the center of several apartment complexes. A wild-looking patch of grey, dried-up plants sits in one square of the yard. Along the borders lie wild, bushy plants. You see a rectangular pool of white concrete full of sky-blue water. You're walking through backyards of condos, definitely trespassing, but no one seems to be around. Dad can be cool sometimes.

You like this place.

Then you wake up.